Michigan Governors: Their Life Stories

Michigan Governors: Their Life Stories

Willah Weddon

NOG Press
325B N. Clippert
Lansing, Michigan 48912

© 1994 by Willah Weddon. All rights reserved.

No part of this book may be reproduced or transmitted in any form or by any means, electronic or mechanical, including photocopying, recording, or by any information storage and retrieval systems, without permission in writing from the publisher, except in case of brief quotations embodied in articles and reviews.

Published 1994
First Edition
Printed in the United States of American

Published by NOG Press
325 B, North Clippert Street, Lansing, Michigan 48912

ISBN 0-9638376-2-1

Library of Congress Cataloging-in-Publication Data
Weddon, Willah
MICHIGAN GOVERNORS: Their Life Stories
First Edition
Governors * Michigan * Short Biographies
977.4/0092 a B

Library of Congress Card Number: 93-87563

Table of Contents

Foreword

We think of Michigan as always having been a part of the United States. But 25 other states had joined the union before Michigan was accepted by Congress as the 26th state in 1837. Then Michigan was represented by the 26th star in the flag of the United States of America.

For as far back as is known, Indians had lived, hunted and fished in this land. When the French came to Canada, they considered what is now known as Michigan as belonging to them. They sent explorers through the Upper Peninsula hoping to find a water route to Asia.

The French explorers didn't find the Pacific ocean, but they discovered that the Indians had many beautiful furs to trade. Word spread and soon fur trappers were pushing westward looking for more pelts to send back to France.

Next came the French missionaries bringing Christianity to the Indians. They were not always successful in converting the natives and suffered great hardships...some of them were murdered. But they drew maps and made reports which were printed in France. This information was a great help to those who came later to this vast territory.

A few missions, settlements and forts were established. Still, it was nearly 100 years after the falls of St. Marys River was discovered before Detroit was founded by a Frenchman, Antoine Cadillac, in 1701. Then, sixty-two years later, when the French and Indian war ended, the First Treaty of Paris gave all the French territory east of the Mississippi River to Great Britain.

Within months, Indian uprisings began to plague the area. They wiped out the garrison at Fort Mackinac and massacred whites in other forts. They besieged Detroit for more than five months, but weren't successful in taking it over.

At the close of the Revolutionary War in 1783 another Treaty of Paris was signed and a vast area that had belonged to the British, including what is now known as Michigan, was turned over to the United States. Four years later Congress set it up as the Northwest Territory and divided what was to become Michigan between the territories of Ohio and Indiana.

It wasn't until 1805 that the territory of Michigan was organized by Congress with Detroit as the capital. Gen. William Hull was appointed governor by President Thomas Jefferson. But a few years later, during the War of 1812, Detroit was the scene of a short skirmish with British troops.

Governor Hull surprised his men by surrendering to the British. They were disgusted with him and Hull was found guilty of cowardice, neglect of duty and unofficerlike conduct. He was sentenced to be shot. President James Madison set aside the punishment and replaced Hull with Brig. Gen. Lewis Cass who was later named territorial governor.

General Cass served as governor of Michigan Territory from 1813 to 1831, when George B. Porter was named governor. Both governors had territorial secretaries who filled in for them as acting governors when they were absent from their posts. William Woodbridge, Gen. John T. Mason and his son, Stevens T. Mason, were among those secretaries who served as acting governors at various times during these years.

The territorial governors and secretaries were appointed by the President of the United States. It wasn't until 1835 that Michigan had it's first elected governor, Stevens T. Mason. He remained in office after Michigan was officially declared a state in 1837.

Mason, and the governors who followed him, were faced with many problems as the new State of Michigan suffered from growing pains and financial panics. They were leaders of our state through the Civil War, World War I and World War II.

Where were these governors born and raised? What influenced their lives and how did they become governors? How did they handle tough situations as Michigan grew and matured as a state? All this is told in the pages that follow.

First Governor of the State of Michigan

Stevens T. Mason
1835-1840

Stevens Thomson Mason was only 18 years old when he came to Detroit with his parents and six sisters. He was born in Virginia, on October 27, 1811. His family had moved to Lexington, Kentucky, when he was a child and he was raised there.

His father, John T. Mason, became a successful lawyer and businessman in Kentucky. Tom, as Stevens was called, attended the University of Transylvania. But when hard times hit and his father's finances went down the drain, Tom had to leave school and take a job as a grocer's clerk.[1]

Loss of the family fortune led Tom's father to accept an appointment by President Andrew Jackson as Secretary of Michigan Territory in 1830. The family moved to Detroit, which was then the capital of the territory.

Young Mason was intelligent, good-looking and had a gentle sense of humor. Being the only son, he spent a great deal of time helping his father with the work of territorial secretary. He became so familiar with the duties, in fact, that he carried on when his father was traveling to other states on business.

An interest in government came naturally for Mason. His great-grandfather George Mason had written most of the "Bill of Rights" for the U. S. Constitution and was a friend of George Washington as well as Patrick Henry. Tom's grandfather had been a U.S. Senator from Virginia.

His father, however, never cared much for politics and resigned his position in Michigan to go to Texas in the summer of 1831, hoping to rebuild the family fortune. He convinced President Jackson to appoint 19 year-old Tom to take his place as territorial secretary.

Part of the secretary's job was to fill in for the governor when he was absent and the idea of a boy, not old enough to vote, running the territory didn't sit well with many citizens. They held meetings and sent a committee to visit Mason and demanded he give up the job.

"President Jackson appointed me with his eyes open—go home and mind your own business," Mason told them firmly. They decided this young man might be able to handle the job after all, but planned to keep a watchful eye on him.[2]

Territorial Governors Lewis Cass and later, George Porter, were gone for lengthy periods of time and young Mason, as acting governor, performed their duties so well that the citizens gradually became his supporters.

During this time Mason studied law and passed the bar exam. He met with the Territorial Legislative Council regularly and promoted his dream that Michigan become a state.

When the Indian agent at Chicago asked for assistance in stemming the threat of an Indian uprising led by Black Hawk and his band in Illinois, Mason took action. He ordered the militia into service and about 300 men were mustered in Detroit and headed for Niles. It turned out that they weren't needed and Mason called them back, but he gained a reputation as a spirited leader.[3]

It wasn't long before Mason convinced the Territorial Council that Michigan's population was greater than the 60,000 needed to qualify it to become a state in the Union. Members of the Council petitioned Congress but their request for statehood was tabled.

Meanwhile, a cholera epidemic hit the territory and Governor George Porter died, once again making Mason the acting governor. He promptly called the Council into special session and proposed they authorize a census to determine the size of the population. Then he told them they should call a convention to form a state government, elect a representative and two senators, and send them to Washington to demand admission into the Union.[4]

The Council agreed with Mason and, when they met early in 1835, ordered an election for delegates and held a constitutional convention in Detroit on May 11. The constitution they drew up is considered by some historians as the best one Michigan ever had. It was to be voted on in October.

Things took a unexpected turn during the summer. The Toledo Strip, along the border of Michigan and Ohio, had been claimed by both states. This issue became heated now that Michigan was applying for statehood.

Acting governor Mason mobilized the territorial militia and placed himself at the head of the troops. They marched into the strip and The Toledo War was ready to erupt.

Ohio's Governor Robert Lucas appointed a sheriff and judges to hold court in a newly created county to establish their claim on the disputed area. They held their meeting in the dark and then rushed for dear life to safety in Maumee. There was only one casualty in the so-called war. A Michigan sheriff was stabbed by an Ohioan with a jackknife in a tavern scuffle. The Ohioan's name was Two Stickney and he was the brother of One Stickney.

Realizing the danger of an armed battle breaking out, President Jackson called Mason a "Young Hotspur" and sent word to him in September that he was being replaced. Mason turned his command over to General Joseph W. Brown, who immediately disbanded the troops.

President Jackson named John Horner of Virginia as the new territorial secretary of Michigan. But by now Mason was exceedingly popular and the people wanted no part of Horner. They chanted a poem, "Johnie Horner, who fled to a corner, and got no Chrismas pie."[5] He did flee as far as Ypsilanti, where a crowd gathered in front of his house and threw stones and blobs of horse dung at it. Later, he was appointed secretary of the new Territory of Wisconsin and high-tailed it to the west.

Although the President had dismissed Mason from the office of territorial secretary in September, the election that had been scheduled earlier was held according to plans. On the first Monday of October, voters approved the constitution and a day later elected Mason their governor...all before Michigan was admitted to the Union as a state.

It wasn't long before he was described as the "boy governor" in an Ann Arbor newspaper. Mason disliked the nickname so much that when he met the reporter on a street in Detroit, he took a few swings at him. But the title stuck.

Mason had another, tougher fight on his hands if Michigan was to become a state. This one called for diplomacy and politics. He recognized that congress wasn't going to award statehood to Michigan until the dispute was settled with Ohio and eventually a compromise was reached. Michigan got the western Upper Peninsula and Ohio retained the 470-square miles in the Toledo strip.

As a result, on January 26, 1837, Michigan was admitted as the 26th state in the Union. Congress recognized the 1835 Constitution and it's elected officials. Thus, Mason remained governor and this time it was legal. He was the first elected governor of the state at the age of 24 and re-elected at age 26.

One of his greatest services to Michigan was Mason's encouragement of a state-directed free school system. He signed bills providing for the location of the University of Michigan at Ann Arbor, requested a state geological survey, encouraged the building of a state prison at Jackson and promoted a plan for improvements within the state.

During his second term in office, the state legislature voted to send Mason to New York to get a loan so the new state could build roads and make other needed improvements he'd promoted. He went to New York, negotiated a $5-million loan and met a beautiful young lady. Her name was Julia Phelps. He returned for their wedding on November 1, 1838, and brought her back with him to Detroit.

Through his years in office up to now, Mason's sister Emily had been a great help to him. She served as his hostess at official events, helped him with his speeches and they were often seen together as they rode their horses along the streets of Detroit.

Now that her brother had a bride, Emily left to travel. Detroit at that time was a boisterous frontier town, filled with rough people. An open sewer ran through it and the roads were either muddy or dusty. Everyone depended on horses for transportation.

Politics were also wild and wooly. The panic of 1837 had hit the country and the loan he'd obtained didn't work out. Banks began to fail and Mason was the scapegoat.

Julia became afraid for her husband's life. She was used to a more refined society and within six months, Mason took her back to New York, returning without her. He made several trips to see her and this took time away from his work as governor.

By the time his term as governor was up on January 1, 1840, Mason had had it. He claimed he was leaving Michigan without any regret and headed for New York. He started his own law practice and tried to support Julia and their three children, Stevens IV, Dorothea and Thaddeus Phelps. After three years he was beginning to make a living, but fell ill and within three days he died. The doctors said his death was caused by "suppressed Scarlet Fever." He was 31 years old when he died on January 4, 1843.[6]

Although Mason was buried in New York, his remains were brought back to Detroit in 1905, more than 60 years later, and reinterred in Capitol Park in downtown Detroit. Today there is a life-size statue of Mason, cast in bronze from melted down cannons from Fort Michilimackinac, standing on the site.[7]

Governor William Woodbridge
1840 and 1841

William Woodbridge, Michigan's second governor, was born in the latter part of the Revolutionary War and lived until after the first major battle of the Civil War. You can tell by looking at his picture that he took things seriously. There wasn't much fun in his life.

His ancestors had settled in Massachusetts in 1634, just 14 years after the pilgrims arrived at Plymouth Rock. They had left England because they weren't about to give up their freedoms of speech or religion.

His father, Dudley Woodbridge, was a graduate of Yale and had served as a minuteman in the Revolutionary War. His mother, Lucy Backus Woodbridge, came from a family that also opposed taking orders from the British Empire. Lucy's mother, in fact, spent 13 days in jail for refusing to pay taxes to New England's established church.

With a background like this, it was not surprising that their son, William, grew up with "an unconquerable aversion to tyranny," as he put it.[1] He never hesitated to oppose things he considered harmful to citizens in a free country.

William was the second son of Dudley and Lucy Woodbridge. He was born on August 20, 1780, in Norwich, Connecticut. He had two older sisters, Lucy and Sarah, and an older brother, Dudley.

When William was about nine years old, his mother, father and two sisters moved to Marietta, Ohio in 1789. William and Dudley were left behind to live with a cousin.[2] His parents felt it was important for the boys to remain in Connecticut so they could continue their schooling.

Two years later, however, William's father made the trip back and brought the boys to Marietta to join their family. William went to school in the town block house and learned some grammar and the multiplication tables. He later spent a year with the French colonists at Gallipolis and learned their language. This was a big help to him when he grew up because he could understand French and he was always sympathetic to French families when they were ill-treated by the British.

Marietta was a growing town in the wilderness and there was considerable anxiety about the Indians in the area who were attacking pioneers. It wasn't until 1794, when "Mad Anthony" Wayne and his troops defeated Tecumseh in the Battle of Fallen Timbers, a few miles south of what is Toledo today, that the families could get on with their lives.

During this time William worked in a law office in Marietta and became a good friend of Lewis Cass. But when he was 16, his father sent him to Litchfield, Connecticut, to continue his studies. He entered Tapping Reeve's academy, the first Law School in America. It was here that he met beautiful, talented Juliana Trumbull who was six years younger than he was. He fell in love.

Although William graduated after three years and returned to Marietta, he corresponded with Juliana for two more years. Then, after he'd built a house for them, he went back to marry her and brought her to Ohio with him on horseback.

There wasn't much business in Marietta for a young lawyer and William Woodbridge was soon into politics. He was elected to the Ohio assembly, held appointive offices and served in the Ohio Senate until 1815. At that time, his old friend Lewis Cass, now Territorial Governor of Michigan, offered Woodbridge the job of Secretary of the Territory and Collector of Customs at the port of Detroit.

Woodbridge decided this was an opportunity he couldn't pass up and President James Madison officially appointed him to the jobs in January 1815. He spent two weeks traveling through the "Black Swamp" from Marietta to Detroit. The swamp was a 40-mile stretch of mire and impossible to ride through in some seasons.

Detroit was newly incorporated as a city, but the British had left destruction in their wake after the war of 1812. The Indians in the area and the French along the Raisin River were out of food and money. William met with the Indian Chiefs and they were friendly at first, but by spring they were saying they wanted their land back. Under a treaty they had given up the area from the Maumee River in Ohio to Port Huron in Michigan. He tried to help them.

Things were not going well for William Woodbridge. As territorial secretary and customs collector, he had enough to do. But Cass left for the summer and he was acting governor, too. Back in Marietta, Juliana had a baby girl in September and didn't want to make the trip to Michigan through the swamp until the baby was strong enough to travel.

Juliana arrived early in 1816, and discovered Detroit wasn't as nice a place to live as Marietta. But they managed. Woodbridge had purchased some land along the river and eventually they had a nice home and orchards, where they raised four of their six children. One baby, John, died when he was 4 months old and a daughter, Henrietta, died when she was 5 years old.

Meanwhile, Woodbridge didn't earn enough with his two jobs to pay his bills and worried about money. He was elected Michigan's first representative to the U.S. Congress in 1819 and went to Washington. Although he could talk, he couldn't vote, because Michigan wasn't a state.

A question was raised concerning his holding two public offices at the same time, both territorial secretary and a representative to congress. His salary was held up so he still had money worries. He represented Michigan as well as he could but returned to Michigan a year later and didn't run for re-election to congress.

Back in his job as territorial secretary, Woodbridge served until 1828, when President John Quincy Adams appointed him a justice of the territorial Supreme Court. He served for four years and and then continued to be active in politics. In 1838 he was elected to the state senate and was very critical of the way Governor Mason handled state affairs.

Woodbridge claimed that because Michigan was not a state when Mason was first elected, he held the office illegally; that Mason should not have let the Toledo strip go to Ohio; and blamed him for the state's financial straits due to the $5-million loan Mason had arranged for in New York. Mason was a Democrat and Woodbridge was a Whig.

A year later (1840), Woodbridge became the first and only Whig governor Michigan ever had. He didn't hold the office very long, though. In 1841 he was elected to the U.S. Senate by the state legislature and resigned his post as governor.

He went to Washington again, this time with a vote and a salary, and served the state well. When his six-year term expired, he did not run for re-election.

Much of his time after he retired was spent in defending his farm from the City of Detroit. As the city boundries enlarged, his taxes were raised and he had to pay for roads built through his own property. He spent a great deal of time in court and was able to hang on to his land until he died on October 20, 1861.

After his death, at the age of 81, the Woodbridge farm was soon taken up by the growing city of Detroit. Today, Tiger Stadium stands on a portion of the land that once belonged to him.

Governor James Wright Gordon
1841

James Wright Gordon was lieutenant governor when Governor William Woodbridge resigned to go to the U.S. Senate in Washington.He automatically became acting governor.

Gordon had a husky voice, due to a defect in his palate, but a friend said that his reasoning was so good that no one noticed the defect after he started talking. "It was a triumph of the reasoning powers over a poor voice," and he became known as a distinguished public speaker.[1]

He was born in 1809, in Plainfield, Connecticut. His father was a Brigade Quartermaster in President John Quincy Adams' army and a politician. The family moved to Geneva, New York, where their children could get a good education.[2]

Gordon took advantage of this opportunity and went on to graduate from college and become a professor at Geneva. While there he studied law and was admitted to the bar. In Geneva he also married Mary Hudun and they had five children: Anna, Catharine, Mary G., Edwin and Alfred.

During Michigan's land rush of 1835, Gordon brought his family to Marshall and started a law practice. He got into politics and was elected to the state senate. Everything was going well for him. He began to dream big dreams.

Gordon introduced a bill to make his town the state capital with land nearby to be the capitol grounds. The young city was located on the road between Detroit and Chicago and the railroad was coming through. He'd been assured by his politician friends that Ann Arbor would get the University, Jackson the penitentiary and Marshall the state capitol.

In 1839 Gordon built a beautiful home for his family, still called the Governor's Mansion, on a hill he called Capitol hill. He undoubtedly had visions of being the governor who would live in that house. For starters, he was popular with his fellow Whigs and elected Lt. Governor. Next he had his eye on a U.S. Senate seat.

About that time, things started to go sour for the ambitious lawyer-politician. When it came time for the legislature to elect a U.S. Senator, some Democrats joined with some Whigs and elected Governor Woodbridge, rather than Gordon. The move left Gordon astounded and the scene "was long laughed over by the politicians in Michigan."[3]

Gordon was governor of Michigan for 10 months and a week. The Governors' mansion was in Marshall but the capital was still in Detroit. (It wasn't until 1847 that Lansing was selected as the site of the capital by the state legislature.) At the end of his term, Gordon returned to Marshall and hoped for a Federal appointment. When he was offered a consulship to Brazil several years later, he went to South America thinking that a change in climate would improve his failing health.

Three years after going to Pernambuco in Brazil, Gordon had a coughing fit and fell off a second-story balcony and died as a result. His body was never returned to the United States and, in fact, his grave has not been located in Pernambuco. Gordon is the only Michigan governor whose gravesite remains unknown.[4]

Note: You can see the Governor's Mansion in Marshall. It has been restored by the Mary Marshall Chapter of the D.A.R.

Governor John S. Barry
1842 through 1846; 1850 and 1851

Although John Steward Barry was born in New Hampshire, January 29, 1802, his parents moved to Vermont when he was young. He had two brothers, Charles and Aldis. He worked on his father's farm and studied by himself until he was 21. Then he went on his own.

Barry married Mary Kidder, of Grafton, Vermont and they moved to Georgia where he studied law while he was in charge of an academy for two years. He was Captain of a company of State Militia, practiced law and became a Governor's Aide.

In 1831, the Barrys moved to White Pigeon, Michigan, and he entered the mercantile business. Three years later they moved to Constantine where he became a successful merchant. He made a lot of money, but with his background in law his interest turned more and more to politics.

He started out as a Justice of the Peace, then became a Judge of Probate and the people trusted him. As the years went by he was a member of the territorial Legislature, a member of the Constitutional Convention, a member of the first State Senate and elected three times Governor of Michigan.

At that time a governor could only serve two consecutive terms, according to the state constitution. But Barry proved such a good governor that after he'd served two terms and retired to Constantine, he was called back for another term. (Meanwhile two other governors had each served one term.) Even though he was not at the Democrat's convention in Jackson, he was nominated and when notified, he accepted. He went on to win the election.

During his first two terms, the capitol was located in Detroit. When he went back for his third term in 1850, the capitol had been moved to Lansing.

The state was in poor financial condition when Barry took office as governor. He used his own money to get a loan so the state could build the Central Railroad through from Marshall to Kalamazoo. It was also said that when the University of Michigan needed money to pay salaries, he advanced the money to save it from being closed.

Barry had always worked hard for his money and he was careful how he spent it. He expected the state to do likewise.

The story is told of how the legislature had voted $500 for services of a secretary to the governor on one hand, but failed to provide $503 for postage needed to call the Constitutional Convention of 1850. Barry insisted a bankrupt state couldn't afford private secretaries and he did the work himself. Then he sold the hay from grass cut on the capitol lawn for $3, added it to the $500 and paid the postage bills.

He was known as a man of strong opinions and few words. When a member of the House asked him if there was some economical way the acoustics in the House chambers could be improved, he replied, "Yes. Talk slowly. Talk sense. Talk as little as possible."[1]

After his third term as governor, Barry returned to his business and his wife in Constantine. They had no children and Mary continued to devote all her time to keeping house and taking care of her husband. She died a year before his death in 1870. They were both buried in Constantine and their home is now a museum.

Note: The Barry home is located at 260 N. Washington Street and is maintained as a museum by the Governor Barry Historical Society and Constantine Community Center.

Governor Alpheus Felch
1846-1847

Alpheus Felch started out in life with the odds against him. Born on September 28, 1804, in Limerick, Maine, he was such a delicate child that his relatives doubted whether he would live to grow up.[1]

When he was only two years old his father died and fourteen months later his mother died. Alpheus, their only son, had five sisters and they were all taken into the homes of relatives.

Alpheus was sent to live with his grandfather, Abijah Felch, for the next six years. When he was about 10 years old his grandfather died, and from then on he lived with his other grandfather Piper or an aunt.[2]

Despite the sad events in his life, young Felch did well in school. He attended the Limerick Academy and was only 17 when he entered Philips' Academy at Exeter, N. H., to prepare for college. After that he spent four years at Bowdoin College and then studied law. He was admitted to the bar at Bangor, Maine, in 1830.

Felch began practicing law in Houlton, Maine, where one of his sisters lived. But his health was still not very good and after three years he was advised by his doctor to move to a southern, warmer climate if he wanted to live through another winter.

Deciding to go to Mississippi, he traveled by stage coach, steam-boat and canal-boat with a stop enroute in Monroe, Michigan. Here he visited Wolcott Lawrence and met his daughter, Lucretia. He went on to Cincinnati, Ohio, but fate took a hand. He became ill with cholera and although he recovered, he decided to return to Monroe until cooler weather.

Felch never continued on his journey. He and Lucretia were married in September of 1837, in Monroe. In the coming years they had eight children, all but one of them growing to adulthood.

While practicing law in Monroe, Felch gained a reputation for his integrity and learning. He was soon elected village attorney and in 1835 to the state legislature. This was followed by appointments to serve as State Bank Commissioner, Auditor General, judge of the Circuit Court and one of the justices of the Supreme Court. He was elected governor of Michigan and before his term was up in 1847, he was elected to the U.S. Senate.

While in Washington, he was successful in getting the government to build the first canal at Sault Ste. Marie. After six years as a U.S. senator, Felch was named to a commission to adjust and settle the Spanish and Mexican land claims under the treaty of Guadalupe Hidalgo. When this work was completed in California, he was offered a job there but turned it down so he and Lucretia could bring their children back to Ann Arbor where they could get a good education.

Felch opened a law office in the city until his retirement in 1874. Five years later he was appointed Tappan professor of law in the University of Michigan and filled the post for five years.

His honesty was revealed during the financial crash of 1837. He had co-signed notes for many people, trusting them to pay. When they went bankrupt, to avoid paying their debts, he told the creditors that if they would give him time he would pay the amounts in full. He did this out of his salary as a U.S. Senator.

"I never knew him to utter a profane, vulgar or uncouth expression or to tell an uncouth story. I never saw him in anger or heard him utter one single unkind word, even in the heat of the trial of causes," his son-in-law, Claudius B. Grant, wrote of Felch.

Although Alpheus Felch was plagued by ill health in his early life, he set a record for living the longest of any Michigan governor. He died in 1896, at the age of 91, in Ann Arbor where he was buried.

Governor William L. Greenly
1847

Wwilliam L. Greenly was lieutenant governor when Alpheus Felch resigned the governorship to become a U.S. Senator. Since there were only 10 months left in Felch's term, Greenly is noted for serving as governor the shortest time in Michigan's history.

Greenly wasn't governor long enough to set much of a record. He was the first one to have three wives, however. One before, one during and one after he was the chief executive.

Born in 1813, in Hamilton, New York, Greenly was raised there and studied law for three years. He was admitted to the bar in 1833 and began practice in New York. A year later he married Sarah A. Dascomb from Hamilton.[1]

Sarah apparently died and Greenly moved to Adrian, Michigan in 1836 where he set up another law practice. A year after coming to Adrian he ran for the state legislature but was defeated. Two years later he ran again and was elected for two terms to the state senate.

Between his terms as a senator, Greenly returned to the East and married Elizabeth Hubbard. They had two sons and the youngest, William M. was born about the time Greenly was elected lieutenant governor in 1845.

On March 3, 1847, Greenly became acting governor when Felch was elected to go to Washington. On March 16, Greenly signed the bill which moved the state capital from Detroit to Lansing. He also supervised the raising of Michigan troops for the Mexican war.[2] When the gubernatorial term was completed Greenly returned to his home in Adrian. He was mayor of the city in 1858 and a year later Elizabeth died.

Described as "a scholarly, cultured and genial man,"[3] Greenly married Maria Hart, a local girl, in 1859. Maria and one of his sons, Marshall, survived him when he died on November 29, 1883, at the age of 70. He was buried in the Adrian cemetery.

Epaphroditus Ransom
1848 and 1849

When he was a boy, Epaphroditus Ransom worked on the hillsides of his father's farm summers and attended school during the winter months. As he grew older he taught the school, although at the time he probably didn't have more than an eighth grade education himself. This was not uncommon in those days.

"Epaphro" as he signed his name at times, was the eldest son in a family of 12 children. Records vary as to when he was born, but his son wrote that he was born on March 24, 1798 and this is confirmed on his tombstone in Kalamzoo.[1]

There is agreement that he was born in Shelburne Falls, Massachusetts, and the Ransom family moved to Townshend, Vermont, when he was young. He graduated from Chester academy and studied law until he could enter Law school in Northampton, Massachusetts. He graduated in 1823 and opened his law practice in his hometown of Townshend.

Family members described Ransom as tall, well-built with dark hair and eyes. He was somewhat reserved, but was friendly to those who greeted him.

Within a couple years Ransom was elected to the Vermont legislature which met in Montpelier, Vermont. It was here that he met Almira Cadwell and they were married on February 21, 1827. They made their home in Townshend where three of their children were born: Wyllys Cadwell, Elizabeth (who died shortly after her first birthday), and Antoinette.

Meanwhile, two of Ransom's brothers and a sister had moved to Michigan and sent back glowing reports of the new territory. Epaphroditus and Almira decided to join them. He closed his business, they loaded their belongings on wagons and headed west with their two young children. It took them a month, by wagon, canal, steamboat and wagon again, to arrive in Bronson (now Kalamazoo) by November 1834.

They lived in a log cabin that first winter, with snow drifting through the roof and wolves howling beneath their windows. But by the next fall Ransom had his law practice well underway and built an office with a house next door to it for his family.

Governor Stevens T. Mason appointed Ransom the first Circuit Court Judge in Western Michigan and an Associate Justice of the Supreme Court. This required a lot of travel by horseback along old Indian trails, and Almira was alone with the children much of the time. They had another baby boy in March 1837, but he died in infancy.

The city of Kalamazoo was growing rapidly all around them so the Ransoms had their house moved to a large farm site where they raised sheep, cattle and had large orchards. In 1843 Governor John S. Barry appointed Ransom the Chief Justice of the Michigan Supreme Court. Four years later he was nominated for governor by the Democratic party.

Ransom won the election, resigned from the Court and was the first governor to be inaugurated in Lansing, now the state capital. The ceremony was held in a two-story frame building known as the State House.

During his two years as governor, Ransom encouraged legislation dealing with the development of the Upper Peninsula and promoted construction of plank roads throughout the state. The asylums of the state were established under his recommendations and he was active in organizing the Michigan Agricultural Society.

He failed to get renominated for the office by his party, partly due to his strong anti-slavery position, and he returned to Kalamazoo. The people in his area supported him, however, and he was elected to the state legislature in 1853-54.[2]

Ransom went into partnership with his son Wyllys and they invested in plank roads and a banking business. The panic of 1855 wiped out the bank and they also lost the money they'd invested in plank roads.

Faced with his financial losses and broken in health, Ransom was grateful when President James Buchanan appointed him receiver of the public monies for the Osage land office at Fort Scott, Kansas, in 1857. The family moved to Kansas but trouble seemed to follow him. He was one of three federal officers whose lives were threatened by pro-slavery forces on the Kansas frontier.[3]

Ransom died at Fort Scott on November 11, 1859.[4] The following January his family brought his body back to Kalamazoo and he was buried there. Almira returned to Fort Scott where she lived until her death in 1877.

Note: Rather than nominate Governor Ransom for another term, the Democrats nominated John S. Barry, who had already served two terms as governor from 1842-1846. Barry won the election and became the first governor to serve three terms. It was legal, according to the constitution, because his third term was not a consecutive one.

Governor Robert McClelland
1852 to March 8, 1853

To look at Governor Robert McClelland's picture, you'd think he was a mighty serious man. But those who knew him thought differently. He seldom told a story or said anything witty, yet friends said he loved to hear others say funny things and laughed easily. In fact, his political opponents accused him of laughing himself into office.

McClelland was born at Greencastle, Pennsylvania, August 1, 1807. His father was a physician and he had good schooling in his early years. When he was 17, however, he was on his own. He taught school and saved his money so he could go to Dickinson College in Carlisle, Pennsylvania. After graduating first in his class, he went back to teaching and studied law until he was admitted to the bar in 1831.

He practiced law in Pittsburgh for about a year and then headed west. He arrived in Monroe, Michigan in 1833 and joined up with John Quincy Adams (who had been President in 1824). They were partners for two years before McClelland opened his own office.

Undoubtedly encouraged to get into politics by Adams, McClelland was elected a member of the 1835 convention to frame a constitution for the proposed State of Michigan. A few years later, in 1837, McClelland married Elizabeth Sarah Sabin from Massachusetts. She was seven years younger than he was and they had six children, with at least three of them living to adulthood.[1]

McClelland was elected to the state legislature in 1838 and to the U.S. Congress for three terms, from 1843 to 1849. He represented Michigan well in Washington and was a friend of Lewis Cass and Alpheus Felch. He was also a good friend of David Wilmot, who was responsible for the Wilmot Proviso, which called for the prohibition of slavery in new territory acquired by the United States.[2]

When he returned to Michigan he was a delegate to the 1850 Constitutional Convention and ran for governor the next year on the Democratic ticket. He was elected in 1851 for a one-year term, as was specified in the newly adopted constitution. He ran again in 1852 and was re-elected for a two-year term.

There were no great acts or problems during his administration. He got the new constitution working well and the state treasury was finally on a solid basis. Actually, McCelland served as governor for little more than a year.

He had just begun his second term in office when in March, 1853, President Franklin Pierce appointed him secretary of interior. He was the third governor in 12 years to resign early and go to Washington. The other two, William Woodbridge and Alpheus Felch, however, had left to serve as U.S. Senators.

It was Lieutenant Governor Andrew Parsons who stepped in to fill the remaining year and 10 months as governor. McClelland served in the President's cabinet for four years.

The McClellands made their home in Detroit when he returned to Michigan. He was a delegate from Wayne County to the 1867 Constitutional Convention in Lansing. In 1870 he made a private tour of Europe. He died on August 30, 1880 and was buried in Elmwood cemetery, Detroit. Sarah died in 1887 and was buried beside him. Two of their six children were still living.

Governor Andrew Parsons
1853 and 1854

G overnor Andrew Parsons was the last Democrat in the governor's office for the next 36 years. Starting with Stevens T. Mason all the governors had been Democrats, except for 1840 and 1841 when the Whigs won the seat.

Parsons had been lieutenant governor only two months (January 1, 1853 to March 7, 1853) when Governor Robert McClelland resigned to go to

Washington as secretary of the interior. He filled out the remaining year and ten months which was almost a full term.

Born in Hoosick, New York, on July 22, 1817, Parsons traced his ancestry back to Ireland in 1290. Not much is known about his childhood, but the good-looking Irishman came to Michigan in 1835, when he was 17 years old. He had at least two brothers, Luke and S. Titus, active in Michigan politics. They probably made the trip here with him from New York.[1]

Parsons taught school for a few months at Ann Arbor and then moved to Ionia County where he was a clerk at Prairie Creek. From there he settled in Shiawassee County where he was soon elected register of deeds and held the post for six years. He obviously studied law during this time, because he was the county prosecuting attorney in 1848.

In those days if a young man wanted to become a lawyer he worked with another lawyer or in a law office and studied. When he thought he knew enough, he could take the state bar examination and if he passed it, he'd be admitted to the bar. In this case, Parsons' brothers were both lawyers.

Parsons was elected a state senator in 1847 and 1848 and in 1852 he became a Regent of the University of Michigan, a post he resigned when elected Lt. Governor that fall.

After assuming the governorship when McClelland left for Washington, Parsons was pressured by the railroad interests to call a special session of the legislature. He wouldn't do it, however, and earned a reputation for being a man of spotless character. He was a good speaker and considered a firm and reliable governor.

Although he was a Democrat, his party members did not renominate him for a second term. The Republican party had been formed "under the oaks" at Jackson in 1854 and the Democrats wanted a stronger candidate to run for governor on their ticket. Parsons did, however, run for state representative from his district and win.

Legislative sessions in Lansing were short then and this one met only from January 3 to February 13, 1855. But Parsons was in "very feeble health" by the time the session ended.[2] He died at his home in Corunna on June 6th, at the age of 37, and was buried in Pinetree Cemetery. His tombstone is a modest marble slab with the seal of the state engraved on it, the only Michigan governor's tombstone to be so marked.

Parsons had married Elvira Howe in 1839 and they had two children before her death ten years later. He then married Anna Marilla Ferrand Stewart who had three children by her first marriage. The couple had two more children, one of them, Andrew E., was born less than two months after Parsons left the office of governor.

Birth of a Party

From the time Michigan was a territory looking to become a state, politics played a major role in the lives of its citizens. They talked and fought about which party was going to run their government.

Early Presidents, George Washington and John Adams had been Federalists. Thomas Jefferson and others following him were known as Democrat Republicans. By 1828, the supporters of Andrew Jackson were known as Democrats and supporters of his opponents, John Quincy Adams and Henry Clay, were known as National Republicans. By 1840, the Whig party was strong enough to elect William Harrison.

Here in Michigan our first governor, Stevens T. Mason, was a Democrat. But when hard times hit the state many voters turned to the Whig party and in 1839 elected William Woodbridge governor. By 1841 the Democrats regained the governorship with election of John Barry and won every state office after that until 1854.

What happened in 1854? The Republican party was formed "under the oaks" in Jackson.

Some of the Democrats had joined forces with the Liberty party, and formed a Free Soil party opposing slavery. Their platform called for "no more slave states, no slave territory, no nationalized slavery, and no national legislation for the extradition of slaves."(1) Some Whigs were also unhappy because their party was not taking a strong stand against slavery.

Convinced the time was ready for a new political party, Charles V. DeLand, editor of a Jackson newspaper, the *American Citizen*...which is today the *Citizen Patriot*...got busy. He worked hard to get people from across the state to come to a meeting in Jackson and organize a new political party.

On July 6, 1854, more than a thousand men (some historians say 3,000) gathered in Jackson in an oak grove. Whigs, Democrats, Free Soilers and Abolitionists cooperated to draw up a platform and stated, "We will cooperate and be known as Republicans..." They nominated a slate of officers, with Kinsley S. Bingham for governor. Bingham had been a

Democrat, turned to the Free Soil party and now was the leader of the new party. In the November election the entire Republican ticket was swept into office.

At least six other men known to have attended the meeting were later elected governors of Michigan. These included: Moses Wisner from Pontiac, Austin Blair from Jackson, Henry P. Baldwin from Detroit, John J. Bagley from Detroit and Charles Croswell from Adrian. Cyrus Luce from Adrian was an organizer, but his presence at the meeting has not been confirmed. David Jerome from Saginaw was not present but he was a charter member.

It wasn't until 36 years later that a Democrat, Edwin B. Winans, was elected governor of Michigan.

Governor Kinsley S. Bingham
1855 through 1858

The first Republican governor of Michigan was Kinsley Scott Bingham and from then until 1932, Michigan voters almost always voted Republican. A lawyer and a farmer, honest and hard-working, he set a good example.

Kinsley was born on December 16, 1808 and raised on his father's farm in Camillus, New York. When he'd completed his basic school work he studied law in the office of General James R. Lawrence.

His life changed when two lassies, Margaret and Janet Warden, came from Scotland to Camillus. Their Uncle Nidean had told them they could have his land in Camillus if they would come to America. Their 17 year-old brother, Robert, followed in 1832. They met Bingham and they all got along very well. So well, in fact, that Bingham and Margaret were married in 1833. Then the four of them drove by horse and wagon through Canada to Michigan, taking the canal to Buffalo.

When they arrived in Livingston County, Bingham and his brother-in-law, Robert, purchased 400 acres in Green Oak township. They began clearing the timber-covered land and built a double log house. It was here that Margaret gave birth to a son, Kinsley Warden, on May 28, 1834. Four days later she died and her sister Janet took care of the baby.

Although Bingham was busy working the land, his background in law was soon put to use. He was elected Justice of the Peace and Postmaster under the territorial government and was the first Probate Judge in the county. He was elected to the first state legislature when Michigan became a state and was re-elected four times.

During this time Robert Warden's parents arrived from Scotland and brought their youngest daughter, Mary, with them. They all lived in the double log house and Mary and Kinsley fell in love. Her mother didn't approve of Mary marrying her dead sister's husband, but they were married on June 10, 1839. In 1840 they had a son, James, who joined the U.S. Army when he grew up and died a soldier in the Civil War.

In 1846, Bingham was elected to congress and re-elected in 1848 on the Democratic ticket. Mary went with him to Washington in November 1849, and wrote home telling about their trip. "We had the company of Gen. Cass and Gov. Felch all the way from Syracuse, and a more agreeable, unassuming old gentleman than the General is, I never saw," she wrote. (Both Lewis Cass and Alpheus Felch were U.S. Senators at that time.)

Strongly opposed to slavery, Bingham had become a member of the Free Soiler Party and had been nominated as their candidate for governor. But

Bingham said he would withdraw his nomination and favor withdrawal of the entire Free Soil ticket, if the other anti-slavery factions would join together in the effort to keep slavery from extending to new territories.[1]

When the historic meeting was held "under the oaks" in Jackson, on July 6, 1854, Bingham was picked to run for governor on the ticket of the newly formed Republican party. He, and others on the slate, were swept into office in November. He was also re-elected two years later.

Much of the focus during Bingham's governorship was on the slavery issue. The Personal Liberty law was passed, providing that all prosecuting attorneys "... use all lawful means to protect and defend all persons arrested as fugitive slaves." The ship canal, at the Falls of St. Mary (now known as the Soo), was completed and connected Lake Huron and Lake Superior.

With the Republicans holding the majority in both houses of the legislature, many laws were passed affecting the growth of mining, railroads and the timber industry. He was credited with placing the State Agricultural College (now Michigan State University) and the State Reform School in operation.

At the close of his second term as governor, Bingham was elected to the U.S. Senate for a six-year term. He took an active part in the election campaign for Abraham Lincoln and he and Mary went to Lincoln's Inaugural Ball in Washington.

But Bingham served in the Senate less than two years. He died suddenly at his home in Green Oak on October 5, 1861. He was buried in a private cemetery on the Bingham farm and his body was later moved to the Old Village Cemetery in Brighton.

Note: The Bingham house has been preserved and the Green Oak Historical Society is in the basement. It is located on Silver Lake Road, between Kensington and Dixboro roads, near South Lyon.

Governor Moses Wisner
1859 and 1860

To those who didn't know Governor Moses Wisner, he appeared to be cold and indifferent. But when he started to speak against slavery and states seceding from the Union, he was a powerful, impassioned orator. He was a man of action, too. When the Civil War started, he led an infantry regiment to Kentucky.

Like many governors before him, Moses was born and raised on a farm in the East. He was born on June 3, 1815, in Springport, New York, and was the 12th of 16 children in the family. Only eight children lived to be more than 14 years old and at least two of them came to Michigan. George, who was two years older than Moses, moved to Pontiac in 1835, studied law and set up a practice there.

The year Michigan gained statehood, Moses was 22 years old. He made the trip to Michigan and bought a farm in Lapeer County. He spent two years clearing and planting the new land before deciding to get on his horse, go to Pontiac and study law with his brother.[1]

After Moses passed his bar exam he returned to the village of Lapeer and was appointed prosecuting attorney for the county in 1841. This same year he married Eliza Richardson from New York, and they had a son, Edward, in 1842.

Business wasn't very good, so Moses moved his family to Pontiac in 1844 and joined his brother's law firm. He purchased a farm and everything was going well until his wife died in July after giving birth to a little girl, who also died a few days later.

Four years went by before Wisner met 20 year-old Angeolina Hascall from Flint. He was 33 years old, courted her passionately and they married in 1848. He kept adding acreage to the farm, now called Pine Grove, and it was here that their three children were born.

Although Wisner and his brother were both Whigs, Moses wasn't involved much in politics until the issue of slavery in the territories became heated in 1852. Then, typically, he went all out. By the time the Missouri Compromise was repealed in 1854, opening the territories to slavery, he was among the first in Michigan to denounce the scheme.

Wisner attended the meeting "under the oaks" at Jackson and was a member of the nominating committee that selected Kinsley Bingham to run for governor on the Republican ticket. Wisner was nominated for a congressional seat by his district but was defeated at the polls. At the legislative session in 1857 he was a candidate for a U.S. Senate seat, but didn't get that either.

In 1858, however, Wisner was nominated for governor on the Republican ticket and won the race. It was his first and only political victory. He was built well, had jet black hair, spoke with conviction and the people believed in him. Today we'd say he had charisma.

During his years as governor, the first law was passed requiring the registration of voters, a system of roads was built extending into unsettled areas in the state and he saw that the St. Mary's Ship Canal was put in good condition.[2]

The governor's annual salary of $1,000 was not enough to provide a home for the family in Lansing, so Angeoline stayed at Pine Grove with the children. She had their parlor redecorated and they did the official entertaining there.

But there was a problem. There was a financial panic in the state and a large sum of money was embezzled by the state treasurer. Although Wisner was neither aware of the latter situation nor responsible for it, a shadow fell on his administration when it was revealed. This may have influenced his decision not to seek a second term.

When he gave his farewell address to the legislature he said, "This is no time for timid and vacillating councils, when the cry of treason and rebellion is ringing in our ears." He continued, " Michigan cannot recognize the right of a State to secede from this Union...we cannot consent to have one star obliterated from our flag."

He returned to his law practice in Pontiac, but the Civil War started right after he left office. In July 1862, Governor Austin Blair needed more troops and appointed Wisner to organize the 22nd Michigan Infantry Regiment. As their commander, Colonel Wisner studied military tactics and saw that 997 men were equipped and trained. Although the camp was less than one-half mile from Pine Grove, he lived in a tent alongside the soldiers.

On September 4, the Colonel and his regiment left for combat in Kentucky. They were in some skirmishes with the Rebels as they moved to winter quarters in October, near Lexington. It was a harsh winter, there was little food and much sickness. In early November, Wisner fell ill with typhoid fever. He stayed with his troops until the 17th. By then he was so sick little could be done to help him.

He was moved to a house in Lexington and died there on January 5, 1863. His body was brought back to Pontiac and he was buried in Oak Hill Cemetery.

Note: Pine Grove, the Wisner house in Pontiac, has been preserved and is owned by the Oakland County Historical Foundation as a center for the Pioneer and Historical Society.

Governor Austin Blair
1861 through 1864

Austin Blair was one of the most dedicated of the anti-slavery spokesmen at the organizational meeting of the Republican Party at Jackson in 1854. And the party campaigned against the extension of slavery from that time on.

Little more than three months after Blair took office as governor in January 1861, the Civil War erupted. He gave whole-hearted support to

President Abraham Lincoln and saw to it that the First Michigan Infantry Regiment arrived in Washington before any other western regiment.

When Blair's second term ended, the Civil War was nearly over and he became known as the "War Governor." He used his own money when necessary and left office a poorer man than when he entered. His statue is standing on the front lawn of the Capitol building in Lansing, in tribute to his efforts.

Blair's great-grandparents had sailed to America from Scotland in 1756, and his grandfather was born on the ship during the trip. His father had cleared land and built the first log cabin in Tompkins County, New York, where Austin was born on February 8, 1818. With this background, it is not surprising that Austin Blair had strong opinions and wouldn't back down when he thought he was right. Sometimes this got him into trouble.

When he went to Cazenovia Seminary to prepare for college, he was one of the protesters against an annual religious revival the students were expected to attend. He entered Hamilton College, but changed to Union College in his junior year and while there he took part in a revolt against secret societies and helped organize an association to check on them. His fearless independence was a trademark throughout his career.[1]

In 1841, Blair came to Jackson, Michigan and in February he married Persis Lyman. He was admitted to the Michigan bar that October and the couple left for Eaton County in 1842. Although he was elected Eaton County Clerk that year, his income was small. In February they had a baby girl who died when she was seven months old and Persis died the following January.

A heart-broken Blair resigned his first political post and moved back to Jackson early in 1844.

He began his law practice again and in 1846 he was elected to the Michigan House of Representatives. In May of that year he also married again. This time to Elizabeth Pratt, but she died on April 28, 1847 and their infant son died when he was four months old.

Two years later he married a widow, Sarah Ford, and fortune smiled on him. They had four boys and one daughter, Nelly. Nelly died when she was 10 months old, but the boys all outlived their parents. During this time the Blairs built a big house in Jackson and he continued his career in politics.

Blair was Jackson County Prosecutor and was a Whig, but switched parties when the Republican Party was formed "under the oaks" in Jackson. He was elected to the state senate for a two-year term in 1855. In January 1861 he became governor or Michigan.

When word came that Lincoln needed troops, the legislature authorized the raising of 10 companies but didn't appropriate the necessary funds. One reason for this was because there wasn't much money left in the state treasury. The treasurer in the previous administration had embezzled it.

Blair took charge. He raised $80-$100,000 through donations from private sources and accomplished the mission. As the war progressed, he did everything in his power to see that the North was the victor.

When a letter was received from the Secretary of War early in 1861, advising Blair not to raise more than four regiments, he ignored it and established a camp of instruction for officers of the Fifth, Sixth and Seventh regiments. In August he sent them out to recruit and organize regiments in the state.

Meanwhile, President Lincoln called for more volunteers and Michigan was ready, sending 21,337 men to the field before the 12th of September. Once again Blair's independence had proved invaluable and he continued organizing and sending regiments to the front. Michigan sent a total of 90,000 troops into the Union forces.

While his dedication was great, so were his expenses. He traveled a great deal visiting troops and raising funds. These costs weren't reimbursed and his governor's salary was only $1,000 a year. He spent so much of his time in the war effort that he couldn't earn extra money in his law practice as other governors had been able to do.

By the end of his second term, Blair was nearly broke, very weary and had a hard time re-establishing his business in Jackson. But there were benefits. Officers of the 10th and 11th Michigan Cavalry gave him huge gilt console mirrors in appreciation of his efforts. Michigan regiments also gave him a fine table with a rose colored marble top and a marble dog under a glass dome for his own special table. The soldiers even gave him lace curtains for windows in the addition he'd built on the house to hold the beautiful console mirrors.[2]

Sarah contributed her share, too, during the war. She spent many hours helping sick and lonely soldiers who were camped near their home in Jackson before leaving for combat. Hundreds of them wrote to her later to thank her.

In 1867, Blair was elected to Congress from his district and was re-elected two times. Sticking to his practice of saying what he thought was right, Blair criticized the Post Office Department, spoke in favor of reforming the Civil Service and, finally, became disgusted with President Ulysses S. Grant's administration. When he left congress in 1872, he supported Horace Greeley for President on the Liberal Republican party, but Grant was re-elected.

Blair was a candidate for governor in 1874 on the Liberal Republican party with Democrats support, but was defeated. After that he stayed out of politics for several years.[3] He was still vitally interested in government, however. His granddaughter Nellie Blair Greene recalled that the family would gather in the evenings in the library. The Governor, as his sons called him, would pace up and down on one side of the table with one of the boys on the other. They would talk, argue, and reminisce while Sarah and their sons' wives sat around the fire with their work.

His granddaughter also told about the green parrot, Loretta, who adored the Governor but made his life miserable. "He never came into the library to read and rest, that the parrot did not say, 'Hello Grandpa!' at the top of her voice. He would come out of his thoughts and say, 'Hello Loretta, now be quiet!' Then she would subside."

Although he would have liked to have been a U.S. Senator, Blair had been outspoken on many issues and hadn't tended his political fences. He'd denied that he belonged to either major political party and was never nominated by the state legislature for the Senate. But by 1880 he was back in the Republican Party and in 1882, members nominated him for Regent of the University of Michigan. He was elected and served until 1890. During this period (1885 to 1887) Blair served as Prosecuting Attorney for Jackson County, having been elected on a People's ticket.

Blair continued in his law office practically to the end of his life and his son, Charles, assisted him. Charles later served one term as Attorney General of the state (1903-1904) and became chief justice of the Supreme Court of Michigan. The other three sons went their own ways. George died in 1903, Fred moved to Washington, D.C. and Austin True lived in New York City.

Blair died on August 6, 1894 at Jackson and was buried in Mount Evergreen Cemetery. Sarah died three years later and was buried there too, alongside his other two wives and their two infants.

The legislature of 1895 appropriated funds for his bronze memorial statue on the Capitol grounds and 120 years after he served as governor he was again honored. Michigan Historical Markers were placed at Blair's former house in Eaton Rapids and in a park in Jackson, which was renamed in his honor.

Governor Henry H. Crapo
1865 through 1868

Within three months after Henry Crapo became governor on January 4, 1865, the Civil War ended. He was just what Michigan needed, a man with a business background who could get the state back into normalcy and solvency after the financial strain imposed by the war effort.

Crapo (pronouced cray-po) was the first of several lumber barons to be elected governor and the first one who had not studied law nor been a lawyer. His inquiring mind led him into many fields during his life, however, and he was successful in them all. He prided himself on talking little but working hard. He was considered a good man by both political parties and didn't let politics influence his policies or appointments.

Born on May 24, 1804, at Dartmouth, Massachusetts, Crapo was the eldest son of Jesse and Phoebe Howland Crapo. They were farmers who tried to eke out a living on very poor soil. His father was of French descent and his mother was a descendant of Resolved White, a member of the original 1620 Mayflower Company.

Things didn't come easy for young Henry Crapo. He had very little formal education. But this didn't stop him from learning. He couldn't afford a dictionary so he made his own list of words and walked seven miles to and from the nearest library to look up the meaning of the words and write them down. By the time he was 18, he'd put all the lists together in a cardboard-bound volume and had his own dictionary.[1]

He located a book on surveying and learned the theory of surveying. When a surveyor's job was available, he couldn't take it without a compass and couldn't afford to buy one. That didn't stop him though. He went to a backsmith's shop, made his own compass and got the job.

Crapo continued his studies until he could teach in the Dartmouth village school. Later, he studied and passed a stiff examination to become the master of a new high school. He was teaching when he married Mary Ann Slocum on June 9, 1825. She continued to live with her wealthy parents at Barney's Joy for several years and weekends he walked 20 miles each way to spend time with her.

Their first two children were born before the couple moved in 1828 to a home of their own in New Bedford. He had made investments in real estate which had begun to pay off. In New Bedford he went back to surveying and, along with his real estate and insurance businesses, auctioneering and whaling interests, he prospered. He held several positions in local government and was a Colonel of a regiment in the State militia.

During these years the Crapos had eight more children. Of ten children, they had one son and nine daughters. They had a beautiful home and were well-off.

Then, in 1856 Crapo decided they should come to Michigan. He'd invested heavily in pine lands and felt they should move to Flint to tend their holdings. Two of their children, William and Rebecca, were grown by then and stayed behind.

Within a relatively short time after arriving in Flint, Crapo had become a lumber baron and more than regained his financial standing. At one time he had as many as five lumber mills in operation simultaneously. He organized the Flint and Holly Railroad and bought a 1,385-acre farm in Swartz Creek. He enjoyed the latter as he'd always been interested in horticulture. He also played an important role in the government of Flint, serving as mayor for one term.

Although Crapo had been a Whig, he joined the Republican party after it was formed. In 1862 he was elected to the state senate and became Chairman of the Committee on Banks and Incorporations and a member of the Committee on Bounties to Soldiers. In the fall of 1864, he was elected governor on the Republican ticket. He was re-elected two years later and held office until the end of 1868.

During the four years he was governor, Crapo was especially firm on three issues.
   A. He insisted the state "pay as we go" and stay out of debt.
   B. He vetoed bills that would have authorized giving financial aid to railroads, saying it was fiscally unsound and that it was unconstitutional for the government to give funds to private business.
   C. He rarely pardoned convicts, pointing out that the court's decisions should be upheld.[2]

While serving his last term, Crapo became ill and suffered a great deal but kept on with his work. He went out of office in January and died the following July 22, 1869. Of the 12 pallbearers at his funeral in Flint, one was Governor Henry Baldwin and two others, David Jerome and Josiah Begole, were to become governors in the future.[3]

Crapo's decision to move to Michigan had an effect on the state in later years, too. It was his grandson, Billy Durant, who founded General Motors Corporation in Flint.

Governor Henry P. Baldwin
1869 through 1872

Young Henry Porter Baldwin was made of stern stuff. He was born at Coventry, Rhode Island, February 22, 1814, and was the 12th child in a family of 15.[1] His ancestors were Puritans who had come to America in the early 1600s and two of his great-grandfathers had been college graduates and ministers. But both his parents had died by the time he was 11 years old.

Although he'd had a New England common-school education, Baldwin had to go to work as a clerk in a store at the age of 12. He clerked and studied in his time off for the next six years. Then he opened his own business and married Harriet M. Day in 1835.

The couple came to Detroit in the spring of 1838 and he started a shoe and boot business and became an influential banker. They had four children and all but one, Jeanie, died in infancy or while young.

Although Baldwin had been a Whig, like many others he'd attended the organizational meeting of the Republican party in Jackson. In 1861 he served in the state senate and was named chairman of the committee to investigate the state treasury. This was the year the Civil War broke out and Governor Austin Blair discovered there wasn't any money for troops because the state treasurer had pilfered the funds during the previous administration.

With his banking background, Baldwin not only investigated but drew up a report with plans for regulating state finances in the future. At the close of his senate term he was urged to run for governor, but declined since it was customary for an incumbent to be re-nominated.

Harriet died on January 24, 1865 and almost two years later Baldwin married Sibyl Lambard or Sibyle Lombard (spellings vary) on November 21, 1866. Sibyl was 25 years younger than he was and they had three daughters; Sybil, Katharine and Marie.

In 1868, Baldwin accepted the nomination for governor and won by the largest majority so far in the state. He served for two terms. He recommended building a new Capitol and when the legislature authorized the funds he saw that contracts were let for construction.

During these years the lumber business was flourishing and the lumberjacks left tops and branches by the acre on land they had cleared. A drought and hot weather in the summer of 1871 had created ideal conditions for fires. The first great forest fire started in Holland that October. The town was wiped out and 300 families were left without any belongings or homes.

Farther north, Manistee also suffered a devastating fire which spread across the state to Lake Huron. It left 18,000 people without homes.

Baldwin personally contributed $156,876 of the $462,106 raised for a relief fund to aid the nearly 3,000 families left homeless.[2] He also gave a great deal throughout his life to the church his family belonged to in Detroit.

He returned to private business after leaving the governorship and the Baldwins built a mansion in Detroit. In 1879 he accepted an appointment to fill a vacancy in the U.S. Senate. He served 15 months but lost his bid for the post in the next election. He died on December 31, 1892 and was buried in Elmwood Cemetery, Detroit.

Governor John J. Bagley
1873 through 1876

John Judson Bagley was a big man with a big heart. He was always willing to help anyone who needed sympathy or money and he loved little children.

One of eight children, John was born on July 24, 1832 in Medina, New York. His father was a tanner and the family moved to Constantine, Michigan, when John was 8 years old.[1]

By the time he was 14, John was earning his own living. He'd attended a branch of the University of Michigan in White Pigeon but left school to take a job as a clerk in a country store in Constantine. After a year he left for Owosso.[2]

A family friend from the days when the Bagleys had lived in New York, Dr. J. D. Barnes, lived in Owosso. Young John went to live with the Barnes and attend school with their children. But he soon left school and became a clerk in a store. Then he made another move.

At 16, heavy-set and large for his age, John Bagley set out for Detroit. He had practically no money but was determined to find work. When he arrived in the big city he liked it immediately and decided this was where he wanted live. He found a job in a tobacco factory and worked there until he was 21. Then he went into business for himself.

Two years later he married Frances Elizabeth Newberry, on January 16, 1855, in Dubuque, Iowa, and she returned to Detroit with him. They lived in a small house and in the following years had eight children: Florence, John N., Frances, Margaret, Olive, Katherine, Paul Frederick and Helen.

During these years Bagley's Mayflower Tobacco Company grew into such a successful business that it was the largest of its kind in the West. He was one of the first manufacturers to use advertising and he made a fortune.

Bagley invested his profits in other business ventures. These included the Michigan Mutual Life Insurance Company, The Detroit Safe Company, and two banks. He was a shrewd businessman and all of these projects were successful.

Although too busy in the early days to enter politics, he served on many boards later on. He was also president of the commission governing Detroit's new metropolitan police department.

Bagley was among the Whigs who took part in the organization of the Republican party and in 1872 was their candidate for governor. He was elected and served two terms. He applied his business background to running and creating an efficient state government.

During his administration the State Board of Health and the State Fish Commission were established. The offices of railroad commissioner and insurance commissioner were set up and banking regulations put into effect. He reorganized the state militia, now known as the National Guard, and was a member of the Detroit Light Guard.

Frances Bagley helped form educational groups for women and they were both active in improving education for children. Bagley reorganized the Boys' Reformatory in Lansing and developed the State Public School for Dependent Children in Coldwater for wards of the state.

After his second term, he returned to his business affairs in Detroit and the Bagley family had an elegant home there. Their daughter Katherine had died just before he became governor and in 1878 they funded a memorial fountain on the lawn of the State School in Coldwater in memory of "Kittie".

In 1881, Bagley was a candidate for U.S. Senator and came within one vote of getting the nomination in the Republican caucus. His health was failing, however, and he and Frances went to California in the hope that his circulation would improve. But he died little more than six months later in San Francisco on July 27th.[3] He was buried in Detroit. In his will he left funds for a huge granite memorial drinking fountain so people could quench their thirst with "water cold and pure as the coldest mountain stream".

Governor Charles M. Croswell
1877 through 1880

By the time he was 7 years old, Charles Croswell's mother and only sister had died. Then, within three months, his father accidently drowned in the Hudson River. It was a sad little boy, indeed, who was put into the care of his Aunt Mary and Uncle Daniel Hicks.

Although Charles Miller Croswell, born October 31, 1825 at Newburg, New York, was left orphaned and penniless, he'd had a good start in life. His father, John, had been a paper-maker in New York City and his mother was Sallie Hicks. Both their ancestors had arrived in America in the 1600s and their families had been prominent in publishing and political fields.[1]

His aunt and uncle brought Charles with them to Adrian, Michigan, in 1837. His uncle was a carpenter and when he was 16, Charles joined him as an apprentice. During the four years he was learning the trade, he was also studying and in 1846 he was appointed Deputy Clerk of Lenawee County. As was common in those days, his position as clerk enabled him to study law and in 1850 he was elected Register of Deeds for two terms on the Whig ticket.

In 1852 he married Lucy M. Eddy and they had five children, but only three survived: two daughters and a son. On December 12, 1868, Lucy fell down a stairway in their home with their infant girl in her arms and died the next day. The baby wasn't hurt seriously and Lucy's parents came to live with the children for the next 12 years.[2]

Croswell made the trip from Adrian to Jackson in 1854, where the Republican party was formed, and was secretary of the convention. A year later he formed a law partnership with Judge Thomas Cooley until Cooley was appointed a law professor at the University of Michigan and moved to Ann Arbor. (Cooley later became Chief Justice of the Michigan Supreme Court and today the Cooley Law School in Lansing is named in his honor.)

During the next few years Croswell was appointed city attorney and elected mayor of Adrian. In 1863 he was elected to the state senate and served two terms. He was a delegate to the 1867 Constitutional Convention and was elected its president.

By 1876, Croswell had gained a reputation as an excellent writer, orator and parliamentarian. He was nominated for governor on the Republican ticket and that fall he won by a large majority. He was re-elected in 1878 and just before his inaugural, he and 25 year-old Elizabeth Musgrave from Eaton Rapids were married. He was 52 and had been widowed for ten years.

During Croswell's administration the "great riot" in Jackson took place when the railroad workers went on strike. He immediately sent in troops and was credited with saving lives and property.[3] Michigan's population had grown to 1.6 million and when he left office on January 6, 1881 he told the legislature that for the first time the state treasury had a revenue "equal to its demands." In short, he had balanced the budget.

After completing his second term as governor, Croswell returned to Adrian where he was president of the Lenawee County Savings bank and bought a majority interest in the Opera House which is the Croswell Opera House today.

He sent his son to New York to buy theater seats for the opera house and wrote him a letter telling him he was taking too much time, costing too much money, and that he had best finish up his business and get back home with the theater seats.[4]

Croswell died six years after leaving office, on December 13, 1886. Three months after his death Elizabeth gave birth to their only child, Salliehicks, and named her after Croswell's mother. Elizabeth gave their home in Adrian to the Daughters of the American Revolution in 1927 to preserve as a memorial to the governor.

Note: In the spring of 1961 a wrecking crew preparing to tear down the carriage house behind the Governor Charles Croswell house discovered an old trunk filled with his papers dating back 100 years.

Governor David H. Jerome
1881 and 1882

David Howell Jerome was the first Michigan governor to be born in Michigan. Up to now, all the other governors were born in the eastern states and moved to Michigan later.

David's mother and father had moved from New York to Detroit in 1827 and David was born there on November 17, 1829. His father and another man built the first lumber mill in the west, on Pine River in St. Clair county. But his father died (March 30, 1831) when David was little more than a year old. His mother took him with her back to their old hometown in central New York.

David was the youngest in the family. His father, Horace, had five children by his first wife and after she died he married Elizabeth Rose Hart, David's mother. They had eight children and several of them remained in Michigan the rest of their lives.[1]

In 1834, when David was about about 5 years old, his mother returned to Michigan and brought him with her. He was raised on a farm in St. Clair County and graduated from St. Clair Academy when he was 16. He did some logging, rafted logs down the river, and chartered a steamer with his brother to carry passengers and freight between Port Huron and Detroit. They made good money but then lost it all on a contract to raise "The General Scott," a vessel that had sunk in Lake St. Clair.[2]

When he was 19, David left for California by way of the Isthmus of Panama and worked for a mining company. He located a claim "Live Yankee Tunnel and Mine" which later proved to be worth millions of dollars for the company.

After a year in California, David Jerome came back to Michigan and started a general store in Saginaw. He changed it later to hardware and it grew into the largest hardware store in the Saginaw valley. He also went into the lumber business with his step-brother and became very wealthy.

In 1859, Jerome and Lucy Amelia Peck were married. Her father was in the lumber business and influential in Oakland County politics. The couple had three children. Two died while infants and the third, Thomas Spencer Jerome, grew up to be a lawyer in Detroit.

Although Jerome wasn't present, he was a charter member of the Republican party when it was formed in Jackson and in 1862 he was elected to the state senate on its ticket. Earlier that same year Governor Blair authorized him to raise the 23rd Michigan Infantry regiment, one of six regiments at that time, and prepare it for duty in the Civil War.

During the six years he served in the senate, the now Colonel Jerome was Military Aide to Governor Crapo and was a member of the State

Military Board until 1873. He helped get a bill passed which created the Soldier's Home at Harper Hospital in Detroit.

Jerome was appointed to the U.S. Board of Indian Commissioners in 1876 and as chairman went with a delegation to visit Chief Joseph of the Nez Percé Indian tribe on a peace mission. They traveled to Portland, Oregon, then to the Blue Hills in Idaho, a distance of 600 miles up the Columbia River.[3]

In 1880 Jerome was elected governor. In his first year in office another disastrous forest fire broke out on September 5, 1881. This time it burned across counties in the Thumb area and some of the residents took refuge in Lake Huron as they fled. Thousands were left homeless and more than 125 people lost their lives. Help was given by the newly organized American Red Cross. It was the first disaster-relief project of the Red Cross and was directed by Clara Barton.[4]

During the years Jerome earned a reputation for taking his time in making up his mind about issues, sticking to his decisions and putting them into effect. While he was governor he insisted the railroads were vital to the growth of the state and construction rapidly increased. He also continued the "pay as you go" philosophy for the state and when he went out of office the state treasury had a balance of more than $2 million on hand.

The Democrats and Greenbackers formed a coalition, calling it the "Fusion" ticket during his term. They defeated Jerome in his bid for re-election. He returned to Saginaw where he was president of the Saginaw Valley and St. Louis railroad and of the Saginaw Street Railroad Company.

Jerome died in a sanitarium at Watkins Glen, New York on April 23, 1896, at the age of 67. His wife, Lucy, was with him when he died. Eleven months later she died in Detroit. They were both buried in Oak Hill Cemetery, Pontiac. Their son, Thomas, died in his early fifties, April 12, 1914, in Capri, Italy.

Governor Josiah W. Begole
1883 and 1884

When he was 21, Josiah Begole headed from New York for the territory of Michigan to make his fortune in the West. He traveled by steamer to Toledo and from there he walked to Jackson and on to Flint. He had $100 with him and he didn't know how long it would have to last. He did know that walking was the cheapest way to get where he was going.

Begole was born on January 20, 1815, in Livingston, New York and was the eldest of ten children. His father had served through the War of 1812 as a non-commissioned officer and his mother's grandfather had served as a captain in the Revolutionary War.

Young Josiah went to school in a log schoolhouse and later attended the Temple Hill Academy at Geneseo, New York. With parents of moderate means and nine younger brothers and sisters, Josiah was on his own when he left for Michigan in 1836.

When he arrived in Genesee County there were only three or four houses in the village of Flint. To earn a living he helped build houses during the summers and taught school the next two winters.

Meanwhile, Harriet A. Miles arrived with her parents, four sisters and two brothers from New York. Josiah began to court her and they were married on April 22, 1839 in her family's log house north of Flint. It was one of the first weddings, if not the first, held in the wilderness area and created quite a stir.

The couple began housekeeping in the woods on new, uncleared land in Genesee Township. They spent the next 18 years working to develop it into a 500-acre productive farm. During this time they had five children: Mary, William, Frank, Charles and a daughter who died in infancy.

While working on his farm, Begole served as a school inspector and Justice of the Peace. He had been a Whig, but his strong feelings against slavery led him into the Republican party when it was organized. In 1856 he was elected county treasurer and held the office for four successive two-year terms, throughout the Civil War.

Begole was active in recruiting and furnishing supplies for the army. He spent a great deal of time looking out for families of the soldiers. His eldest son, William, was killed in the war near Atlanta, Georgia by a confederate bullet in 1864. It was one of the greatest sorrows in the life of the Begoles.[1]

As the years went by, Begole became a founder and owner of one of Flint's largest sawmills. He got into banking and manufacturing and eventually became a wealthy businessman.

In 1871, he was nominated and elected a state senator and served one term. Then he was elected to the U.S. House of Representatives and was in Washington during 1873 and 1874. While in Congress he voted for the issuance of large amounts of paper money and became known as a "Greenbacker."

He returned to his businesses in Flint until the Greenback and Democrat parties joined to form a Fusion party and he was their candidate for governor in 1882. He was the only Fusionist ever elected and the oldest man, at 68, ever elected governor of Michigan.

Begole was also the first non-Republican to be elected in nearly 30 years. But he only served one term. He couldn't get much legislation he wanted passed by the legislature because it was controlled by the Republicans. Gridlock existed even then. When he ran for re-election in 1884, he lost by only 3,953 votes to Republican Russell Alger.[2]

Returning again to his business interests in Flint, Begole remained interested in political affairs. When he died on June 6, 1896, Governor John T. Rich pointed out that Begole was one of those who helped redeem our state from a wilderness.

Governor Russell A. Alger
1885 and 1886

Although three other Michigan governors had also been orphaned at an early age and grown up to be highly successful men, Russell Alger did it all. He was a true war hero, became a multi-millionaire lumber baron and was elected Governor of Michigan. He came close to getting the nomination for President by the Republican party. He served as U.S. Secretary of War and was a U.S. Senator when he died.

Russell Alexander Alger was born in a log cabin at Lafayette, Ohio on February 27, 1836. Both his parents, Russell and Caroline Alger, died when he was 11 years old and he was left with a younger brother and sister to look after.[1] (Some accounts say he was 12 years old.)

Life must have looked grim indeed for young Russell. He found homes for his brother and sister and went to live with an uncle. His uncle gave him a room, board, clothes and three months of schooling a year for working on his farm.   He became a farm laborer when he was 14. He earned $3 the first month, $4 the second month and $5 for the next four months. After seven years he was earning $15 a month during good farming weather.

He saved the money he earned and used it to pay his tuition during winter terms at the Richfield Academy all these years. Then he found a job teaching in a district school and could afford to help his brother and sister through school.

When he was 21, he began the study of law in offices in Akron and stayed there until 1859 when he passed the Ohio bar exam. He moved to Cleveland then and joined a law firm for several months.

After years of hard work, study and very little money to live on, Alger's health began to fail. He decided to move to Grand Rapids, Michigan, and try his hand in the lumber business. He did well at first but when the national economy slumped he went into debt.

During the two years he was in Grand Rapids he met Annette Huldana Henry; a slender young woman, intelligent and attractive. She was 19 and he was 25, when they were married in her parents home on April 2, 1861. Within weeks the Civil War was underway and by August, Alger had left to become a private in the Second Michigan Volunteer Cavalry.

When Alger's regiment was mustered into the United States service, on September 2, 1861, he was commissioned captain of the 2nd Cavalry. He was promoted to Major in April 1862. On July 1, he was wounded in action. He was taken prisoner the next day in the battle of Booneville, Mississippi and escaped later that day. In October he was promoted to Lieutenant Colonel of the 6th Michigan Cavalry and his regiment was sent to the Army of the Potomac.

The following February (1863) he was promoted to Colonel of the Fifth Michigan Cavalry and his regiment was in Custer's famous Michigan Cavalry Brigade. A month later, on July 8, 1863, Alger was wounded in the battle of Boonesboro, Maryland. He resigned with an honorable discharge on September 20, 1864.[2]

He had been in 66 battles and skirmishes and was awarded brevet promotions to brigadier and major general in the U.S. Volunteers for his "gallant and meritorious services during the war."

During the winter of 1863-64 Alger was on private service to President Lincoln. He received orders personally from the President and visited nearly all the armies in the field.[3]

When he returned from the war, Annette and Russell moved from Grand Rapids to Detroit and he re-entered the lumber business. This time he was so successful that his R. A. Alger and Co., became the most extensive pine-timber firm in the west. He also built railroads and developed iron industries. By the mid-1880s Alger was a multi-millionaire.

Although he had no political experience, Alger's views were in line with the Republicans and in 1884 he was elected a delegate to the Republican national convention in Chicago. That fall the state party nominated him for governor and he won the election over Fusionist Governor Begole by slightly less than 4,000 votes.

During the years the Algers had nine children but only six of them were living when he took office as governor. The six were Fay, Caroline, Frances, Russell Jr., Fred and Allen.

Alger's administration was run on a business-like basis and the state remained financially strong. The Soldiers Home for veterans was founded in Grand Rapids and the State Board of Pardons was established.

The philosophy that made him a successful businessman didn't change when he became governor. He told the legislators that strikers should realize their only true friends were the men who gave them employment so they could support their families. And he didn't hesitate to send in the militia when a strike occurred in Saginaw Valley. On the other hand, Alger contributed large amounts of money to projects to help the poor.

When his term ended, Alger refused to run for re-election. The family returned to Detroit to live in their new, handsome mansion on Fort Street. He did attend the Republican national conventions, however, and in 1888 he was the leading nominee for president until the sixth ballot. Then it went to General Benjamin Harrison. He was also a popular candidate for nomination in 1892.[4]

President William McKinley appointed Alger to his cabinet as Secretary of War. He served from March 4, 1897 until he resigned in August 1899, after considerable criticism. He had inherited problems with supplies for soldiers during the Spanish-American War and bore the brunt of the inefficiencies. The New York Post reported later, "He was a victim of the wretched organization of the army and the department, which clung to the system of the Civil War that had long been outgrown."

The people gave him a rousing welcome when he returned to Detroit and Governor Hazen S. Pingree defended his work as Secretary of War. While thanking the crowd, Alger said, "I am glad to be among you again… and I propose to stay here the balance of my life." But it was not to be.

Three years later, on September 27, 1902, Governor Aaron T. Bliss appointed Alger to fill an unexpired term in the U. S. Senate and the following January the state legislature elected him to a full term.

For their travels, the Algers had a private railroad car, the "Michigan." They lived in a beautiful house in Washington and entertained many famous people.

Alger didn't complete his term which would have ended on March 4th, 1907. He had suffered from chronic valvular disease of the heart for a long time and died from heart failure on January 24th, in Washington, D.C. His funeral services were held in the Alger mansion in Detroit and nearly 20,000 people lined the streets enroute to Elmwood cemetery where he was buried.

Note: The Grosse Pointe War Memorial was donated by the family of Russell Alger, Jr., son of Governor Alger, who took over the family lumber fortune and became one of the Midwest's leading financiers.

Governor Cyrus G. Luce
1887 through 1890

The past three Republican governors had been wealthy lumbermen/businessmen and the party was feeling the need for a change if they were to win another election. The farmers were gaining strength in the state and Cyrus G. Luce filled the bill perfectly.

He'd been active in the Republican party since it was organized in 1854 and there was no question about his being a farmer. He kept his own horse and cow at Lansing and did the chores himself while he was governor.[1]

His ancestors were Puritans and among the first settlers in Massachusetts. His father had fought in the War of 1812 and later moved to Ohio. Here he met a girl from Virginia. They married, began to dig out a home from the stump-laden soil and had six boys. Cyrus Gray, their second son, was born on July 2, 1824.

The boys all worked on the land and walked along a blazed trail to a log schoolhouse in the woods. When Cyrus was 12, the family moved to Steuben County, Indiana. After two more years of country schooling, Cyrus entered the Academy at Ontario, Indiana. He worked summers and drove a freight team to and from Toledo to earn tuition money. He had to study early in the morning and late at night to keep up with his classes. After three years, he finished his schooling.[2]

Luce began working for his father when he was 17, in the cloth-dressing and wool-carding business. After seven years he was in charge of the factory. When he was 24, his friends nominated him for a seat in the Indiana Legislature on the Whig ticket. Naive about politics and with very little money, he lost the election.

It may have been the aftermath of defeat that convinced Luce to cross the state line to Michigan in 1848. He bought 80 acres of uncleared land in Branch County, near Gilead. In August 1849, Luce married a local girl, Julia A. Dickinson, and they lived in a small frame house he built while developing their farm. They had five children during this time: Elmira J., Emery G., Dwight (who died in infancy), Florence A. and Homer C.

It wasn't long after the couple had set up housekeeping until Luce was taking part in local politics. He was a member of the county board of supervisors for 11 years. He was active in organizing the Republican party and was elected on their 1854 ticket to the state legislature for one term.

He was county treasurer from 1858 to 1862, and elected state senator for two terms in 1864 and 1866. In 1879 Luce was appointed state oil inspector and continued for three-and-a-half years. He was very interested in the farmers Grange movement and was master of the State Grange for many years.

Julia died at the age of 52, on August 1882, after 33 years of marriage. Luce was good-looking, dressed neatly, and was about medium height and sturdy. Within a year he met Mary Brown Thompson, a young widow 19 years his junior, and they were married on November 8, 1883.

Luce's name was entered as a nominee for governor in 1884, but Russell Alger won the nomination and the election. When Alger refused to run for a second term, however, Luce was nominated by acclamation. He was elected governor in 1886 and re-elected in 1888.

Luce and Mary moved to Lansing, where they rented a modest house and lived simply during his years in office. They were the first to spend an entire summer on Mackinac Island.

His administration was "clean, honest, just."[3] He supported legislation to aid farming and watched the state spending carefully. Whether or not the railroads should get tax dollars and how much they should be regulated, had been a bone of contention among legislators and governors for years. Luce believed the railroads should comply with the law but not be crippled. He wanted to protect the peoples' rights and do no injustice to railroads.

Luce also went the extra mile to investigate matters he thought needed attention. He checked the financial records of institutions, investigated every complaint of wrongdoing against officials and listened to pleas from inmates in institutions. He once spent three days traveling to determine whether a prison inmate deserved a pardon. (And found out he didn't!)

When his four years as governor ended, Luce and Mary returned to Coldwater. They bought a house in town where he could oversee his Gilead farm and his business interests. These included the Southern Michigan National Bank, (he'd been a director more than 25 years) and the Coombs Milling Company of which he was president. He and his son, Homer, also had an interest in Hugh Lyons and Co., in Lansing.

By now, Luce's children by his first wife were grown. Elmira was married and lived in Indiana. Emery and his wife kept on with his father's farm. Homer was a successful business man living with his wife and daughter in Lansing. Florence never married but she and Mary were inseparable companions all their lives.[4]

Luce died from heart failure on March 18, 1905, in his home at Coldwater. He was 80 years and 8 months old. He was buried in Oak Grove cemetery. A Memorial Exercise was held for him in April by State Legislators in Lansing and he was highly praised.

Governor Edwin B. Winans
1891 and 1892

V oters seemed satisfied with a farmer governor, so in 1890 the
Democrats nominated a farmer on their ticket… Edwin Baruch
Winans. He won the election but didn't move to Lansing like
Governor Luce had done. He returned to his farm in Livingston County
as often as he could and soon was called the "Farmer Governor."

Edwin was an only child, born May 16, 1826 in Avon, New York. His
parents moved to Unadilla Township in Michigan, when he was 8 years

old and settled on a farm there. His father died, however, and he moved with his mother to Pettysville, four miles west of Hamburg.

Young Edwin found work in a wool-carding and dyeing company and continued his education as best he could. When he was 20, he entered Albion College and spent two years preparing for law school. But he never made it. Gold fever hit him and he left in 1850 for California.[1]

Although he didn't strike it rich with a gold mine, he made money in a company that sold water by ditching it to miners for their operations. After two years he and a partner opened a bank in the mining town of Rough and Ready. They bought gold from the miners and sent it to the mint. It paid off well and in 1855 he headed back to Michigan to marry the girl he'd left behind. She was Sarah, one of six children and the oldest of four daughters of George and Susan Galloway, pioneer farmers near Hamburg.

Sarah had expected to marry Edwin Winans, but she didn't like the idea of leaving home for California or living in a little mining town.

"Take Lib," Sarah said, pointing to her youngest sister with a laugh when he asked her to marry him and head west.[2]

Winans knew Lib (Elizabeth) as well as Sarah, so he proposed to her. She was 19, ten years younger than Winans, and she accepted his offer. They were married on September 3, 1855, and soon left for California.

Their first son, George G., was born in Rough and Ready and they lived there about three years. Elizabeth wanted to return home, though, so Winans sold his business in 1858 and they made plans to sail through the Panama Canal to New York.

They had to bring their money with them in gold coin and this posed a problem. Winans carried the coin in two stout satchels and wore a Colt's revolver on his hip. Elizabeth sewed some of the coins into a dress but discovered after one day that it was just too heavy for her to wear. When they arrived in New York they exchanged the gold for bank credits which made the rest of the trip easier.

After arriving in Michigan they lived with the Galloway family for a time and Winans made another trip west. He and two partners from

Howell and Hamburg shipped supplies to St. Joseph, Missouri. Then they hauled them across Nebraska and Wyoming to Idaho by covered wagons and ox teams. They sold their goods, as well as their wagons and oxen, and headed for home by stagecoach.

Aware of danger from Indians, the men carried arms along the route. Winan's muzzle loading shotgun was heavily charged with buckshot and when the stagecoach accidentally overturned, he was thrown to the ground and his gun discharged. Buckshot hit his right breast and arm, leaving serious wounds. He was taken by covered wagon to the next stage stop. His partners went on but he had to remain behind for several months until he could travel again.[3]

By the time he arrived home, Winans had had enough adventure. He decided to become a farmer. His father-in-law had died and Winans bought the 400-acre farm from the eldest Galloway son. He had much to learn about farming and it wasn't easy. While pushing a boulder from the roadway to help neighbors, he strained an eye so severely that it had to be removed. Few people ever suspected that he wore a glass eye.

It wasn't long before Winans was into politics. He was elected to the Michigan House of Representatives in 1860 and re-elected in 1862. Then he returned to the farm, leaving only to take part in the 1867 Constitutional Convention.

About 1869, Winans and Sarah built a new house on a site overlooking the lake on their farm which came to be known as Winans Lake. He hauled lumber for the house from Flint, some 40 miles away, with horses pulling the loads. It was a beautiful home when it was finished and they lived there for the rest of their lives. It was here that their second son, Edwin B., Jr., was born.

In 1876, Winans decided to run for judge of probate on the Democrat ticket because, he said, he'd like to have a handle to his name before he died. He won the election but was glad when his four year term was over. He found being a judge was monotonous and he didn't like having to stay indoors so much.

In the fall of 1882 Winans was a delegate to the Democrat's convention to nominate a candidate for Congress. Prospects of a Democrat winning were not promising and no one wanted the nomination. Finally, his name was proposed and a friend seated behind him held his coattail so he couldn't get up and decline. He was nominated by acclamation and the convention quickly adjourned. He campaigned hard and won the election by a small margin. He was re-elected in 1884.

In 1890, the Republicans nominated a candidate for governor who was not very popular with their party members. He was James M. Turner, a Lansing railroad baron. The Democrats seized the opportunity and picked Winans as their nominee. So many Republicans supported him that he won the election and Winans became the first Democrat governor in 40 years.

Winans was of medium height and weighed about 200 pounds. He was even-tempered and had a keen sense of humor. The only time he was known to use a swear word was when a man wrote several times asking for money if he'd get votes for Winans. When he was turned down, the man wrote and threatened to take votes away from Winans if he didn't pay him some money. Winans wrote back:

"Sir: I have your letter demanding money, and before I will send you one cent, I'll see you in hell farther than a pigeon can fly in a week."

During his two-year administration, Governor Winan's chief aim was economy. When the legislature appropriated $30,000 to help Detroit entertain the Grand Army of the Republic's encampment, he returned the bill. He said the people of the state in general could not rightfully be taxed for a project which would benefit only Detroit.

He favored tax reform, a general road building program and electoral reform. Although he failed in his bid for tax reform, he was highly respected by his opponents. His eldest son, George, served as his father's private secretary while he was governor and later moved to Montana. Edwin Jr. graduated from West Point and was a Brigadier General at Fort Clark, Texas at the time of his mother's death in 1926.

Winans didn't seek re-election and retired to his farm. He died 18 months later, on July 4, 1894, at the age of 68.

Governor John T. Rich
1893 through 1896

John T. Rich was a large man who probably would have preferred raising sheep, but spent most of his adult life in public service.

He was born in Pennsylvania on April 23, 1841 to John and Jerusha Treadway Rich. They moved to Vermont when he was 5 years old and the next year his mother died.

Father and son came to Michigan a year later (1848) and settled on land which they cleared and began to farm in Elba Township, Lapeer County. His father married Anna Winship, the eldest in a family of nine children that had arrived in Atlas Township from New York in 1837.

Little John attended the district school, the academy in the village of Clarkston and the public schools in the village of Lapeer. As time passed he continued farming. Then he married his stepmother's sister, Lucretia, who was five years older than he was and had been teaching in the local schools.

In 1867 or 1868, John Rich ran for county supervisor on the Republican ticket and was re-elected three times. He was the youngest member of the board of supervisors but was soon recognized as the ablest and was made its chairman.

From this start, his political career rose rapidly. He agreed to run for a seat in the Michigan House of Representatives in 1873 and was re-elected three times, serving two times as speaker of the house. In 1881 he was elected to the state senate but resigned before his term expired to become a member of the U.S. Congress, serving until 1883.

Governor Cyrus Luce then appointed him Commissioner of Railroads from 1887 through 1891. His name was entered for the nomination to run for governor three times, but he didn't get the nomination until the third time in 1892. Then he won the election and served two terms as governor of Michigan.

Rich and Lucretia never had children and she accompanied him when he was holding offices in other parts of the country. They always considered their farm in Elba as their home, although it was run by a nephew and they only had an office and a bedroom there, "just a place to hang their hats." Still, they returned to it whenever they could.[1]

It was here that Rich could supervise care of his Merino sheep. He had breeding stock brought in from Vermont and was recognized as an expert in wool. He served on the national commission which selected wool samples for the customs house authorities from all ports in the world, served as president of the Merino Sheep Breeders' association and as vice-president of the National Wool Growers' association.[2]

Although he was known as a farmer, and this was politically correct at that time, Rich also had interests in lumber and insurance companies.

During his years as governor, the world-wide financial panic of 1893 occurred and affected Michigan. Banks closed, mines closed and thousands were unemployed. These were troubled times but Rich gained the confidence of the people by his actions. Some of the politicians didn't like him, though.

The state canvassing board declared an amendment had passed when it had actually been defeated. The amendment increased the salaries of certain state officers. Rich investigated and promptly gave three of them the boot. The secretary of state, state treasurer and state land commissioner were all removed from office.

After leaving the governorship, Rich was appointed collector of customs in Detroit and later in Port Huron. Between these jobs, he was appointed state treasurer by Governor Fred Warner. Warner had removed a treasurer from office when it was discovered that money was missing. Rich got things back in shape within a few months.

During this time Lucretia became ill and stayed with a sister who lived near the train depot in Elba. This made it easier for John T., as he was called, to come and go while taking care of his government jobs. Lucretia died on May 21, 1912.

Lucretia's niece, Georgia, was a spinster without means and Rich married her nearly four years later. A descendant of her brother, Sam Painter of Davison, recalls that Georgia was "probably the most strong willed woman I ever knew."

The couple made their home in Lapeer and spent their winters in Florida. It was here in St. Petersburg that Rich died after a short illness on March 28, 1926, a month before his 85th birthday.

Governor Hazen S. Pingree
1897 through 1900

They called him "Ping" and he was a rambunctious character. Hazen Pingree had strong ideas about helping the common people and they loved him for it. He thought he could do more for them by being mayor of Detroit and governor of Michigan at the same time. It took a ruling by the state Supreme Court to convince him he couldn't hold both jobs, so he resigned as mayor.

Hazen Senter Pingree, the fourth child of Jasper and Adaline Pingree, was born August 30, 1840, on his father's farm near Denmark, Maine. Young Ping helped on the farm and went to a country school until he was 14. Then, with less than eight years of formal education, he left home to go work in a cotton factory.[1]

In 1860 he got a job as a shoe cutter in a shoe factory in Massachusetts. But the Civil War broke out and in 1862, Ping enlisted as a private in the 1st Massachusetts Regiment of Heavy Artillery. After three years he re-enlisted and served until August 1865.

During this time he was in many battles and was captured by a squad of Mosby's Raiders on May 25, 1864. He spent the next five months as a prisoner of war in Georgia's infamous Andersonville Stockade. After he was exchanged, he rejoined his regiment and took part in more battles all through the rest of the war until Lee's surrender at Appomattox Court House. (April 9, 1865)

When he was mustered out of the Army, 25 year-old Pingree returned home and then came to Detroit. He found a job working in Henry Baldwin's boot and shoe factory. Baldwin had been a state senator and a few years later (1868) was elected governor of Michigan, so Pingree learned something about politics as well as making shoes.

In 1866, Pingree and a partner bought a small boot and shoe manufacturing company of their own, forming Pingree and Smith. While their business was growing into one of the largest of its kind west of New York, Pingree began building a huge stone mansion on Woodward Avenue and found a wife.

He married Frances Gilbert, a 32 year-old school teacher in Mt. Clemens, on February 28, 1872. The couple had three children. Gertrude was born in 1874, but died while a teenager; Hazen Jr., called "Joe," was born in 1877 and Hazel was born in 1880.

As his wealth increased, the Pingree mansion became a showplace of expensive furnishings and the leading businessmen in the city were their friends. When the Republicans needed a candidate for mayor, they urged Pingree to run for the office and he was elected in 1890. To their surprise, he immediately started making reforms to help the common man and it wasn't long before the Pingree's found they no longer had any friends.

"Old Ping," was rotund, 5-foot-8, with sharp blue eyes, a mostly bald head, a mustache and a long beard. He had eyeglasses on a thin gold chain, often wore a bow tie and a black Prince Albert coat with gray trousers. Frances was a beautiful, gentle woman but strong in her opposition to the use of alcohol, tobacco or profanity. Life with Ping, who did not share her opinions but respected them, was far from peaceful. When he brought his father to live them it added to her consternation.

Frances was shocked by the roughness and intensity of politics and gradually withdrew into the seclusion of their home. By the time Ping became governor, she no longer went with him on his official appearances. She wanted no part of politics.

The depression of 1893 left many people in the city in dire straits. Pingree hit upon the plan of getting vacant lots for them to use for planting their own gardens. He became known as "Potato Patch Pingree," and while some people laughed at the idea, it helped supply food for many of the needy and the idea was copied throughout the nation.

Pingree was elected to four terms as mayor and he brought many changes to the city. When he found the people were being cheated and robbed by powerful corporations controlling the gas, light and telephone utilities, he took them on. He decreed a three-cent fare for the horse-drawn rail car lines, lowering it from five-cents. He even had a city owned power and light plant constructed to create competition and reduce public rates.[2]

These actions and his habit of calling a spade a spade, made him unpopular in his own party and members blocked his efforts twice when he wanted to run for governor. Still, they knew the people would vote for him and when they needed votes from Michigan to win a presidential election, they nominated Pingree for Governor. As a result, both he and President William McKinley were winners in 1896.

When Pingree took office in January 1897, he still had a year to go as mayor of Detroit. This was fine with him. He thought he could handle both jobs and get more done. In March, however, the Michigan Supreme Court ruled that he had to give up one or the other. He resigned as mayor. But he never moved to Lansing. He had an office in his home and spent weekends doing state business there.

During Pingree's first term as governor the United States was in the War with Spain. Michigan was asked to send five regiments of volunteers. Pingree established a camp at Island Lake, near Brighton, and lived there with the Michigan troops during the summer of 1898.

He visited the regiments at Chickamauga, Georgia, and demanded better food for them from the War Department after he discovered they were living on hardtack and salt pork. He sent nurses to a camp when he learned they were needed. And, after the war, he sent special trains to carry the sick and wounded back to Michigan. He knew what it was like to be a soldier and did everything he could to help the men.[3]

Meanwhile, in the capitol, Pingree set about to remedy matters in the state. He believed, like other governors for the previous 20 years, that the railroads should pay property taxes. He called the legislature back into session time and again trying to accomplish this goal and nearly succeeded. It wasn't until the next governor took office that they finally passed a railroad-tax law, but Pingree deserved the credit.

Many of his reforms, including a general law for direct primary election and home rule for cities, were not approved either. Some of his goals were at least partially accomplished, such as more equal taxation and more scientific appraisal of corporation properties. He was ahead of his time and fighting all the way.

Toward the end of his second term, a scandal involving a Kalamazoo company was exposed and although Pingree knew nothing about it, his enemies made it look bad for him. A dummy company had been set up to purchase surplus military uniforms at a very low price from the state and turn them over to a parent company where labels were changed. Then the uniforms were sold back to the Michigan quartermaster at full price.

The businessmen confessed and paid back the money. Several state officials involved, however, were sentenced to prison terms. Pingree didn't think they'd been treated fairly and pardoned two of them on the condition they repay the state the money they'd received.[4]

This didn't sit well with the Ingham County Judge who had done the sentencing. He held Pingree in contempt of court. This didn't sit well with old Ping, either, and he left to hunt elephants in South Africa. The Lansing State Republican, carried a quote: "What can you do with a man who, when he is cited to answer a charge of contempt says: 'To hell with your court and your contempt' and sails off to Africa?"

In his farewell address to the legislators, Pingree told them, "In regard to my being locked up for contempt to the Ingham County boy judge, he owes an apology to the people of Michigan for insulting their Governor."

Among other remarks aimed at the legislators, he said, "I am satisfied that I could have had the praise and support of the 'best citizens' and our 'best society,' and of the press of the state generally, if I had upheld those who have for years attempted to control legislation in their own interests, to the end that they might be relieved from sharing equally with the poor and lowly the burden of taxation."[5] It was a long sentence, but it fully expressed his philosophy.

Pingree sent word back from Africa that he had killed his elephant. Then he went on to Germany where he became ill. Friends took him to London but he died there on June 18, 1901, at the age of 60. His body was brought back to Detroit and his funeral was the largest one in the history of the city. A statue was erected in his honor memoralizing him as "Idol of the People."

Governor Aaron T. Bliss
1901 through 1904

After four years with Governor Pingree at the helm, many of the Senators in Lansing were relieved to have Aaron Bliss move into the executive office on January 1, 1901. He was a wealthy lumberman and they assumed he'd be more conservative. They were surprised when Bliss announced in his inaugural speech that he favored Pingree's railroad tax. He wasn't as conservative as they'd hoped.

They'd been through a long fight, however, and the new governor was of a quieter nature. There was less friction under the capitol dome.

Aaron Bliss was born May 22, 1837, in Madison County, New York, the seventh son of Lyman and Anna Bliss. He was raised on the family farm and was a student in a little red schoolhouse nearby. At 17 he left home and worked as a clerk in a store for 14 months and was paid $100. From there he went to Bouckville where he became a junior partner in a store at the age of 20.

"The war came and we settled up and had about enough to pay up our debts, that was all," he recalled later.[1] He enlisted as a private in Co. D, 10th New York Cavalry on October 1, 1861. By the time his regiment left Elmira, he was a first lieutenant and about a year later he was made a captain for gallant conduct on the field of battle. He spent three years and five months in the service, six months of this time as a prisoner of war.

After futile attempts to escape from several prisons, Bliss escaped from the Columbia, North Carolina prison on November 29, 1864. He spent 18 days and 19 nights, traveling through the woods trying to find the Union lines. By the time he located General Sherman, near Savannah, Georgia, he was nearly starved. He later rejoined his regiment and resigned from the army in February 1865.

When Bliss arrived in Saginaw late that September he was still in ill health from his months in the Confederate prisons. He was about five-foot, nine inches in height, had brown eyes and his dark brown hair and mustache were starting to show gray.[2] He was called "Cap" Bliss, stood erect with military bearing and was noted for his lack of a sense of humor.

Bliss found work as a roustabout in a lumber camp on the Pine River. He drove teams, sawed lumber and even did the cooking at times. He saved his money and the next summer he bought four horses and an ox. That winter he took a small job of cutting and drawing timber.

"I worked about a year and a half, I think, and then I heard of a mill at Zilwaukee that was about to go under mortgage foreclosure," he later recalled.[3] He raised the down-payment of $3,000 and was to pay $500 a month until the $20,000 total was paid. That was a lot of money in those days and it was a struggle.

On March 31, 1868, he went back to New York and married Allaseba Phelps, whom he'd known since childhood. They returned to the lumber camp and she pitched in to help by keeping boarders until the business was paid off and profitable. Then they moved to Saginaw and built a huge house in 1873. Bliss joined his brother, Dr. Lyman Bliss and J. H. Jerome (a half-brother to former Governor David Jerome) in a logging company. He added salt, banking, mercantile and farming to his enterprises and became very wealthy. During these years he served on local boards in Saginaw County and in 1883 was elected to the state senate.

When Russell Alger, another Civil War veteran and lumber baron, was elected governor in 1885, he appointed Bliss a member of his staff with the rank of colonel. Then, in 1888, Bliss was elected to the U.S. Congress.

The couple had no children and Allaseba went to Washington for two years with her husband. When they returned, Bliss campaigned for governor and was elected in 1900 and re-elected in 1902.

As governor, Bliss was considered vacillating and weak in many ways and dogged in others. Publicity was a terror to him. He appeared to seldom use his own good judgment and was horrified to be known as a millionaire, for he was constantly pestered for contributions. His instinct for business was excellent, but he was a poor judge of human nature and paid for it many times.[4]

It is little wonder that Bliss did not like publicity. A Chicago Tribune reporter was covering the visit of President Theodore Roosevelt in Detroit, to honor Michigan veterans of the Spanish-American War. The reporter wrote that Gov. Bliss of Michigan was a handsome old man, with a white mustache, but he "should never try to make a speech."

According to the story, "... the governor began his speech by saying, 'Look at Teddy.' As he spoke a peculiar and by no means pleased expression came over the rugged features of the president... he does not enjoy being called 'Teddy' to his face in a public way and by a man who is a comparative stranger. Fortunately for Gov. Bliss, the leader of the band was just then seized with an inspiration to play something... "

Good speaker or not, Bliss knew his business. He insisted on economy in government and the state was free from debt when he left office. He also supported legislation that permitted voters in three counties to hold primary elections for certain offices. Passage of the law was a result of the public outrage over the more than $500,000 that was spent in the 1900 Grand Rapids convention to secure the nomination for governor. There were four candidates, three of them millionaires, and Bliss had won. Chase Osborn, the fourth candidate, was far from being a millionaire at the time.

Never in robust health, Bliss suffered a stroke about a year after leaving the governorship. He was in a sanitarium at Milwaukee, Wisconsin, for treatment for a heart condition when he died, September 16, 1906, at the age of 69.

Governor Fred M. Warner
1905 through 1910

It had been a custom, but not a law, that a governor served only two consecutive terms. Fred Warner was the first to break this precedent when he was elected to a third term.

He was also Michigan's first foreign-born governor. Fred Maltby was born July 21, 1865 in Nottinghamshire, England and his parents brought him to the United States when he was three months old. An older brother remained in England with relatives, but two daughters and Fred, their youngest child, were with their parents when they settled on a wooded farm in Livonia Township.

Fred's mother died and his father put the girls out to live with nearby farm families. Fred was only seven months old and Rhoda Warner said they could bring him to their house for a week on trial. By the end of the week, Rhoda and her husband, Pascal D'Angelis Warner (who was called P.D.) decided he was going to be their boy and they adopted him.[1]

The Warners were well-to-do. P.D. was a successful merchant in Farmington and served in the state legislature. They built the largest house in the village when Fred was 4 years old and it later became his. (Today it is the Farmington Historical Museum.)

Fred graduated from high school and attended Michigan Agricultural College, now Michigan State University, for one term. Then he returned home and began clerking in his father's store. By the time he was 21, in 1887, his father turned the store over to him and the following year he married a local girl, Martha Graft Davis. They had five children. An infant born in 1890 who died, Susan Edessa, Howard Maltby, Harley Davis, and Helen.

After Susan Edessa was born the elder Warners turned their big house over to Fred and Martha. The Warner's loved children and it was a happy, active household. They had one of the first victrolas in town and that attracted a lot of young people. Years later Edessa said she couldn't remember her mother ever being cross.

In 1889, Warner decided to go into the cheese business and opened his first factory at the edge of the family's 250-acre farm on the edge of Farmington. By 1906, he had more than a dozen other cheese factories in operation and the Fred M. Warner Cheese Company became the Warner Dairy Company. He had the milk pasteurized before distributing it and was given credit for safeguarding the public health.

While the family and the cheese businesses were growing, Warner was climbing the political ladder. He was village president and then a state senator for four years, through 1898. A big campaign was on in 1900 with three millionaires vying for the nomination to run for governor on the

Republican ticket, so Warner wisely decided to go for the post of Secretary of State. He won the nomination, was elected and re-elected in 1902 for two more years.

While he was Secretary of State, people became familiar with Warner's name and when he ran for governor in 1904, he was elected by 54 percent of the vote. When he ran for re-election he won by 59 percent, but it dropped down to 48 percent for his third term. In the first election Warner defeated Woodbridge Ferris, a Democrat from Big Rapids, who became governor eight years later.

Mid-way through Warner's second term in office, the Chelsea State bank declared bankruptcy on December 2, 1907. This came as shock to Warner because State Treasurer Frank P. Glazier was president of the bank and had deposited more than $685,857.79 of state funds in it. Glazier wouldn't see anyone and said he was too ill to answer questions. Warner went to Glazier's house in Chelsea to get him to resign but he refused. It wasn't until charges were pressed that Glazier finally resigned on January 22, 1908.

Warner appointed former governor John T. Rich to get things back in order. At the close of Warner's second term in office, however, the state was half-million dollars in debt.

The state's financial situation improved during his third term. For one thing, the bonding companies had repaid all but $167,907.24 of the amount which had been misappropriated by Glazier.

Although Warner was a conservative, he gradually became a leader in the demand for changes. In 1908 the revised constitution was adopted and it contained some progressive features that Governor Pingree had so vainly fought for. Laws were passed placing heavier taxes on railroads, telephone and telegraph companies; regulating insurance companies, conservation, food inspection, child labor laws and direct primary elections for certain offices.[2]

When Warner went out of office he claimed that in no similar period in the history of the state had so much beneficial legislation been provided for the general welfare. He was right.

Governor Warner had been in state politics for 16 years and had been ill at various times during his six years as governor. When he left the office he returned to Farmington where he tended his farming and business interests. But he continued to suffer from uremic poisoning and he died on April 17, 1923, at age 57, in a sanatorium in Orlando, Florida, where he'd gone for treatment.

Governor Chase S. Osborn
1911 and 1912

Chase Salmon Osborn was the first and only Michigan governor who was both a newspaper reporter and publisher. He was the only governor from the Upper Peninsula. He was also one-of-a-kind: an aggressive, capable, colorful man who marched to his own drummer.

He was born in a log house, January 22, 1860, in Huntington County, Indiana. His father, George, and his mother, Margaret Ann, were both physicians and his mother was one of the first women doctors in the United States.

Osborn, with seven brothers and sisters, was independent to the point of being a runaway boy. While going to school in Lafayette, he sold newspapers and learned to set type as an apprentice in a print shop. He got printers ink in his blood and after he spent three years at Purdue University, he returned to work at the *Lafayette Home Journal.*

From there he moved to the *Chicago Tribune* for a short time and then he went to the *Milwaukee Sentinel* in Wisconsin. As a reporter, he had a reputation for running, not walking, on assignments and for carrying a hatchet in his belt.[1]

It was in Milwaukee that Osborn met Lillian Jones and they were married on May 7, 1881. "Our wedding trip was on a streetcar," he recalled later. He was earning $12 a week and Lillian's wedding bouquet was a five-cent one from the German market.

A year later Osborn bought the *Mining News* in Florence, Wisconsin, on the Michigan border and he made it pay well enough so he could buy the *Sault Ste. Marie Evening News* in 1887. The family moved there with three children and had four more in the years to come. (One infant son died and two daughters died before they were 5 years old.)

While running the paper at the Soo, Osborn was appointed the state fish and game warden by Governor John T. Rich in 1894. He was appointed state railroad commissioner by Governor Hazen Pingree in 1899. He and "Ping" got along very well and he learned some political lessons from the old pro. In 1900 Osborn was appointed to the University of Michigan's Board of Regents.

During these years Osborn was extremely interested in politics and decided to make a run for governor in 1900. At the nominating convention, however, reality struck. Of four candidates, Osborn realized he was "just a poor boy in competiton with three millionaires". He claimed later that some of the delegates were offered as much as $3,000 for a vote in the convention.[2]

Osborn got the message. If he wanted to be governor, he had to have big money. So for 10 years this was his goal. He sold the *Evening News* and in

1902 purchased part of the *Saginaw Courier-Herald*. The following year he tramped the wilds of Ontario and discovered the "Moose Mountain," iron range. He sold iron deposits to mining companies and parlayed his money into a fortune.

By this time, however, the 1909 primary law had passed and the candidate for governor was elected by a vote of the people. But money still helped. Osborn had enough of it now so he could run a well-heeled campaign and won the nomination and election in 1910.

"Chase Puts Ginger in the Campaign," some editors remarked. The Detroit News stated on February 10, 1910, "Chase's manager should see that he takes a rest. He kicks and throws bricks at everyone."

One of his campaign promises was that he would only serve one term as governor, so he could spend all his time working for the state rather than campaigning for a second term. He kept his promise.

He also promised to run an efficient, economical administration. He kept this promise, too. When he came into office the state was half-million dollars in debt and when he left, there was a surplus of nearly half-million dollars in the state treasury.

Like Pingree, Osborn battled with the conservative "Immortal 13" in the senate over appointments and other matters, calling the legislature back in special sessions when they didn't follow his recommendations. He got the first workmen's compensation law passed and also a law regulating the "booze" interests, as he called the liquor manufacturers and distributors.

Osborn made friends and he made enemies. He could not be controlled by the party bosses and relished his fights with them. Years later he said he'd had the time of his life while governor. He was considered by many as Michigan's outstanding governor in the past 50 years.

While he was governor he returned for a visit to the Indiana town where he grew up. One of his old German neighbors shook his hand saying, "Is dis der real Chase Osborn?" Then added, "Vat, ain't you been hanged yet?"[3]

One of Osborn's friends was Senator James T. Milliken, father of William Milliken. Osborn and young Bill wrote to each other and he encouraged Bill to go into public service. (William Milliken became governor in 1969.) He was also a friend of another future governor, Fred Green from Ionia.

After leaving the governorship, Osborn traveled all over the world. He was nominated to run again for governor in the 1914 campaign but he was gone during most of the time. His opponent, Democrat Woodbridge Ferris, was re-elected. He also made unsuccessful bids for the nomination to run for U. S. Senate in 1918 and 1930.

In the last 20 years of his life, Osborn led a move to have Isle Royale become a national park and lived to see it established. He also worked to have a bridge built between lower and upper Michigan, but his attempt to get federal funding for it through the Public Works Administration in 1936, was turned down.

In later years Osborn was separated from his wife, Lillian, and spent the rest of his life with his adopted daughter, Stellanova Brunt Osborn. She'd written to him when he was a Regent and she was a student at the University of Michigan. They'd corresponded and met three years later. Innovative as ever, Osborn adopted her in 1931 so they could travel and work together. He was 71 and she was 37. She collaborated with him in his writings and they wrote close to a dozen books.[4]

When he was in his 80s, Osborn liked to live in his camps at Possum Poke, Georgia or Duck Island in the Upper Peninsula, where he could sleep outdoors on a bed of balsam boughs. He gave most of his wealth away to colleges and universities.

Within a year after Lillian died, Osborn had the adoption annulled and he and Stella were married on April 9, 1949. Two days later he died at the age of 89 and was buried on his beloved Duck island.

Governor Woodbridge N. Ferris
1913 through 1916

He was tall and slim with an erect bearing and always stood out in a crowd. Woodbridge Ferris was an educator who claimed he wasn't interested in running for a political office. But he was a smart politician. He waited to run for governor until the odds were in his favor. Then he became the second Democrat to be elected in Michigan since the Republican party was formed 42 years earlier.

One of eight children in the family, Woodbridge Nathan was born on January 6, 1853, in Tioga County, New York. He later wrote of his parents struggle to clear 70 or 80 acres of land for their home and the log cabin they built. "… great trees were cut into logs, rolled into heaps and burned. Gradually the forest disappeared and fields of wheat, patches of corn and buckwheat planted. A few cows and sheep were cared for to eke out a meager existence."[1]

Woodbridge started going to the district school when he was four years old and boredom led him into mischief, with the result that he got frequent floggings. As he grew older he trapped woodchuck and hunted small game with his father's old smooth-bore, muzzle-loading musket.

When he was 14, he entered Spencer Union Academy in the nearby town of Spencer and he had a hard time. His clothes didn't fit well, his manners were different and the village children made fun of him. On top of all that, his teacher called him a blockhead because he was poor in grammar. He was glad to leave the school when he was 16 and enter Candor Union Academy. Here he roomed and cooked meals with a friend, Ed Snyder who later became a sucessful physician in central New York.

Woodbridge always remembered the time he and Ed were struggling to adjust lengths of stove pipe in their room and he said, "Ed why don't you get mad like me?"

"I can't afford to," Ed said, and Ferris never forgot that lesson. He learned to hold his temper and not waste his energy.

When Woodbridge was 17, he attended a Teacher's Institute and passed the exam for a teacher's certificate. With this he could teach in a country school. As was the practice in those days, he earned $28 a month, plus room and board at the homes of his pupils.

By teaching winters and working on a farm summers, he paid his tuition for a course at the Oswego Normal and Training School. It was here that he met Helen Gillespie and fell head over heels in love with her. In the fall of 1873, Ferris came to the University of Michigan and studied in the Medical Department. In the spring, however, he returned to his hometown and got a job in Spencer Academy. He and Helen were married on December 23, 1874 and then she taught in the academy, too.

The young couple dreamed of starting their own school and a year later they organized a business college in Freeport, Illinois. But starting on a shoestring wasn't easy and Ferris took a job he was offered with the Rock River University in Dixon, Illinois. Their first son, Carlton, was born (1876) in the university dormitory.

They tried again to organize a business college, this time at Dixon, but two years later moved to Pittsfield, Illinois, and stayed for five years. Their second son, Clifford, was born here (1881) but died when he was only three months old.

In 1874, Ferris and Helen came to Big Rapids, Michigan, and started the Ferris Industrial School. With two rooms and 15 pupils, he taught and she was the sole assistant. Their dream was coming true. The only entrance requirement was a willingness to study. They taught commercial courses, teacher training and pharmacy, as well as the usual high-school subjects.

The school grew rapidly and nine years later the foundation was laid for the first building on campus. The following year (1894) it became Ferris Institute. During this time their third child, Phelps, was born in 1889. (By 1928 enrollment was up to 2,000 a year, the institute became Ferris College and today it is Ferris State University.)

As his school grew, so did Ferris' reputation as an educator and a businessman. On the business side, he was president of the Big Rapids Savings Bank continuously from the time it was organized in 1894.

Democrats knew a good candidate when they saw one. They nominated Ferris for a congressional seat in 1892, but he was defeated. They nominated him for governor in 1904 and he lost again.

Eight years later the Republicans were split when the Progressive Party was formed. Ferris was quick to realize the possibility of a victory for the Democrats. He accepted the party's nomination for governor and this time he won. He was re-elected two years later.[2]

During his governorship, the legislature was controlled by Republicans but Ferris was more committed to principles than politics and got along well with the legislators most of the time. He liked to study people rather than confront them, but considered himself a natural born fighter to secure reforms.

Like Governor Osborn before him, Ferris believed women should be able to vote in elections. "I want to give women the same chance to make mistakes in public affairs as men," he joked. He also said, "… there is no reason a woman should throw away her brains when she marries."

Helen stayed in Big Rapids the four years he was in Lansing because she wasn't well. He wrote to her daily, however, and relied on her advice. She died on March 23, 1917, less than three months after he left office as governor.

They had a large farm near Big Rapids where Ferris raised registered cattle and did gardening. The flower garden was a show place in the summer and he loved to work in his vegetable garden. He did all the planting and cultivating himself and said it was great exercise.

In 1920 Ferris re-entered the political scene as a candidate once more for governor, but lost the election. A year later he married Mary Ethel McLoud from Indianapolis, Indiana, who was also interested in politics. In 1922 he began a rugged campaign for a seat in the U.S. Senate. He traveled all around the state, made lots of speeches and smoked big black cigars.

By this time there were graduates of Ferris Institute all over Michigan. They joined to support him, Democrats and Republicans alike. A Washington correspondent for the Detroit News, Jay G. Hayden, traveled with Ferris through the state during six weeks of his campaign for the senate seat. Hayden was impressed with the number of former students who turned out in even the smallest towns to greet the teacher they loved and respected.

Hayden pointed out that Ferris had built up a following of his own through the years in this usually solid Republican state. Ferris won the election at the age of 69, and went to Washington in 1923. He was the first Democrat Senator elected from Michigan in more than 60 years. Although he made only one speech, that being in favor of prohibition, he relied on using common sense and was known for his honesty.

Ferris prided himself on never missing an appointment or going to bed with an illness since he was 21. This may have been his downfall. He kept a speaking engagement in Toledo, Ohio in January, although he'd been ill and his physician had advised him to stay home in Washington.

When he got back he insisted on attending every session of the Senate until he finally developed pneumonia and had to give up and go to bed. Within a week, on March 23, 1928, he died at age 75. (His first wife, Helen, had died on that same day in March, just 11 years earlier.)

His widow, Ethel, ran for various political offices after his death. But the $250,000 estate left by Ferris was wiped out by the 1929 depression and poor investments. Before her death in Detroit on February 5, 1954, Ethel had been an indigent patient at the county hospital for six years.

Governor Albert E. Sleeper
1917 through 1920

They called him "Uncle Bert" Sleeper and he was a hard-working governor who appeared to be easy going. He was governor during World War I which lasted nearly two years (April 6, 1917 to November 11, 1918) during his four years in office.

Only Austin Blair was given the title, "War Governor," because he was governor during the Civil War. But Michigan sent troops to fight in the

Spanish-American War under Hazen Pingree, in World War I under Sleeper, and in World War II under Murray Van Wagoner and Harry Kelly.

Albert Edson Sleeper was born at Bradford, Vermont, on December 31, 1862, the son of Joseph Edson and Hannah Sleeper. He studied at Bradford Academy and came to Lexington, Michigan, shortly before his 22nd birthday (1884) to work in his uncle's dry goods store.

He started out as a buyer/manager and a traveling salesman but was soon into banking and the real estate business. Within the next 16 years he became president of banks in Yale, Bad Axe, Marlette, Ubly, and of a wholesale grocery company in Bad Axe.

Sleeper got into local politics and after serving as president of Lexington Village several terms, was nominated by the Republicans for the state senate. He was elected in 1901 and re-elected in 1903.

While in the senate he married Mary Charlotte Moore from Lexington on July 30, 1901. They moved to Bad Axe soon after and lived there for the rest of their lives.

The Sleepers had no children, but practically raised a boy and a girl, Phoebe and Stevens Clark, who lived with them for years. Their father had come from Vermont to visit Bert and died while he was in Michigan. He was only 44 years old and left a widow and four children, so the Sleepers did all they could to help. Stevens drove for "Uncle Bert" when he was governor and they sent him to the University of Michigan. Phoebe and Mary were always close and in later years Mary was like a grandmother to Phoebe's children.[1]

In 1908 Sleeper was elected state treasurer and re-elected in 1910, serving with Governor Fred Warner and Governor Chase Osborn. He kept the books straight, which was a welcome relief for both chief executives.

During these years Sleeper traveled back and forth to Bad Axe on the train. At home he was active in the Episcopal church, a 33rd degree Mason, and virtually every organization in towns where he had business interests. He was also active in the Republican party and in 1916 he was their winning candidate for governor.

He promised in his campaign to bring business methods into state affairs and put a practical budget system and uniform accounting system in place. He also promised to provide "a dollar in service for every dollar in taxes."[2]

Before he could get these reforms in effect, however, war with Germany was threatening. Sleeper called a meeting of state officers to plan action if it should become necessary. The War Preparedness Board was set up and the legislature approved Sleeper's request for a loan of $5 million to be used to organize the Michigan troops.

Their fears were realized. Less than four months after taking office, on April 6, 1917, war was declared and Sleeper plunged immediately into managing military and supply operations by the state. The organization of Michigan Troops was necessary because the National Guard units had been sent to the Mexican border in June 1916. They were sent to help in the hunt for Pancho Villa who had been been raiding the United State's boundary.

(A future governor, Wilber Brucker, was in Mexico with the National Guard. Another future governor, George Romney, had fled as a 5 year-old with his family to safety in Texas from Pancho Villa a few years earlier.)

To protect the state from saboteurs or lawless elements, Sleeper organized the Michigan State Police to help local officers preserve law and order. This became a permanent force.[3] He also purchased 1,000 tractors on his personal responsibity to distribute to farmers so they could produce needed food supplies.

Mary Sleeper went with the governor on many of his trips to build morale and inspect troops. They visited Camp Custer, near Battle Creek, when it was completed in September 1917. Drafted men had arrived from all over Michigan and Wisconsin. "Such a sight, 8,000 men working and 2,000 officers," Mary wrote in her diary.

The influenza epidemic was a tragedy in 1918. Henry Jones, Oakland County, was a boy at the time and recalls a neighbor returning from a trip to Camp Custer. The neighbor had gone to bring his dead son home and he said so many soldiers had died of the flu that their bodies were stacked up like cords of wood in a building.

Things were bad around the state, too. There was a shortage of coal and food. A woman in Bad Axe was arrested for buying 300 pounds of sugar. Entire towns were virtually closed to prevent the spread of influenza.

But on November 11, 1918, the war ended. Peace was declared and glorious celebrations were held throughout the nation. Sleeper was elected for a second term only a few days before the armistice and spent the remainder of his years in office returning the state to normalcy.

He initiated the state park system and the Public Utilities commission. When he left office, he'd kept his campaign promises and believed he'd left the affairs of the state in good shape.

Sleeper returned to Bad Axe where he and Mary had built a large new home in 1916 and continued with his business and political interests. Ordinarily a tolerant man, he'd been very disturbed when his successor, Republican Alexander Groesbeck unfairly criticized his administration. As a result, he began working hard for an anti-Groesbeck candidate and was satisfied when Fred Green won the governorship in 1926. By then Sleeper had become the leader of the conservative wing of the Republican party.

Early in 1932, Sleeper's health began to fail and he died on May 13, 1934, at the age of 71. The depression had hit hard. Known as one "who never could see a neighbor in need without giving aid, a banker who never foreclosed a mortgage... " he had perhaps been too kindhearted. He'd co-signed notes for many people without hesitation and when they didn't pay, it was up to him to make the payments.

Mary used huge amounts of her own money to pay off the remaining notes after his death. She died when she was 91 years old and their home in Bad Axe was sold. It is now a funeral home.

It wasn't until about 50 years later that the city replaced the ground level marker on Governor Sleeper's grave with a monument in the Lexington Municipal Cemetery.[4]

Governor Alexander J. Groesbeck
1921 through 1926

This Republican governor was no personality contest winner and he played political hard ball. He was a successful administrator and he got a lot done, but he stepped on many toes along the way. He was a clever politician although he managed to make many enemies in both Republican and Democrat parties. He was accused of trying to be a one-man government and that was one of the nicer things said about him.

Alexander Joseph Groesback was the second Michigan-born governor, the second to serve three successive terms, the first governor to seek nomination for a fourth term and Michigan's first bachelor governor.

Alex, as he preferred to be called, was born in Warren Township, Macomb County, on November 7, 1872 or 1873. State records and church records disagree. He was baptized in the St. Clement Roman Catholic Church.

His grandfather was the first permanent settler in what is now Warren Township. His father, Louis, was a sawmill owner but when he was elected Macomb County Sheriff in 1880, the family moved to Mt. Clemens where Alex went to school.

Young Groesbeck also attended school at Wallaceburg, Ontario, while his father worked for a lumber company for two years. When he was 13, Alex began working in a sawmill and was there until he was 17. Then he got a job clerking in a Port Huron law firm.

He was intelligent and could see the benefits in becoming a lawyer. He entered the University of Michigan law school in 1892, and graduated in July 1893. The next step was opening an office in Detroit and Groesbeck soon established himself as a brilliant trial attorney.

Although his father was a Democrat, Groesbeck was aware of the advantages in joining the Republican party which had virtually complete control in the state at the time. He began his political career in 1912 and became the state Republican party chairman.

Only two years later, Groesbeck was eager to win the Republican nomination for governor, but he lost out to former Governor Chase Osborn... who lost the election to Woodbridge Ferris. Groesbeck learned fast, however, and when the next state election came around he ran for attorney general. With his experience and support in Wayne County he won the post in 1916 and again in 1918.

While he was attorney general, Groesbeck did a lot of investigating. He revealed prison labor being employed by private businesses, exposed vice and lawlessness in Hamtramck, and brought attention to poor conditions in the State Industrial Home for Girls in Adrian.

He appeared more interested in the publicity for his work than he did in correcting the situations he uncovered. He made it look bad for Governor Sleeper and others in his own Republican party.

After four years of publicity from his investigations as attorney general, Groesbeck ran for governor in 1920 and won in a landslide.[1] He had no problem at first with the legislature because they were all Republicans.

A bachelor, with no family, he spent long hours in the governor's office. He didn't care about social events, either. When other governors were inaugurated they would have receptions and balls. Not "AJ." He would slip in the rear door of the capitol on New Year's Day, take the oath of office and leave. The next morning he would be working at his desk.

Although he had no business training, he ran the state government like a business executive. Upon his recommendation the legislature created the State Administrative Board. The Board drew up a budget for guidance in legislative appropriations, set up a centralized purchasing system, and devised a uniform accounting system for all state agencies. Some state departments objected.

Groesbeck was lucky, though. A Corporation Franchise Tax was levied which brought in nearly $5,500,000 on its first collection in July 1921.[2] And, although he had to agree to a tax on gasoline to get the legislature to approve a centralized highway plan, this paid off for him, too. He was credited with getting Michigans cars "out of the mud," for the 2,000 miles of state highways constructed while he was governor.

The tax also helped with the state finances. No one seemed to know for sure how, or if, the budget was balanced and the people began to demand a look at the books.

During the latter part of his Groesbeck's six years in office, opposition began to mount. He was respected for his competency, but not liked very much and certainly didn't fit the pattern of most politicians. He wasn't friendly and Democrats compared him to Mussolini. Members of his own party called him dictatorial and some had been working to oust him since he first took office.

By the time he sought the nomination to run for governor the fourth term, Groesbeck had burned too many bridges behind him. He'd had a falling out with his good friend, John Haggerty, who controlled the politics in Wayne County. Haggerty joined the opposition and as one newspaper put it, "The much vaunted Groesbeck machine proved a wonderful flop..." [3]

Fred Green from Ionia got the nomination and went ahead to win the 1926 election. Groesbeck did not give up easily, however. He sought the nomination for the governor's seat two more times before deciding to never again be a candidate for office.

Returning to Detroit, Groesbeck continued his law practice and devoted efforts to his numerous business enterprises. He supported several Democrats in future elections. He was appointed chairman of the State Civil Service Commission in 1941, by Democrat Governor Murray Van Wagoner. He died on March 10, 1953 at the age of 79.

Governor Fred W. Green
1927 through 1930

Fred Green loved the outdoors so much that his portrait hanging in the capitol building was painted with him wearing his hunting clothes. He was a sportsman who loved hunting, fishing, raising horses and would go miles to see a boxing match.

He had a happy disposition and had a good time being governor of

Michigan. But he took politics seriously and played for keeps.[1] Alex J. Groesbeck, who preceded him in the governors' office, would vouch for that.

Green's love for the outdoors probably stemmed from being raised in Cadillac, where the land was wild and open. He was born in Manistee on October 20, 1872. His father, Holden N. Green, was a lawyer and lumberman, and his mother was Adeline Clark Green. They moved to Cadillac a year after Fred was born.

Fred went to school in Cadillac and after graduating from high school in 1890, left for the State Normal at Ypsilanti where he earned his B.S. degree and a life certificate to teach. He got a job working for a Republican weekly, the *Ypsilantian*, and liked it so much he stayed for two years. Then he entered law school at the University of Michigan.

While going to classes and selling insurance to pay his way, Green was also dating a student at the university, Helen Kelly. They'd known each other in high school and now began making plans for their future together. But first she graduated and returned to Cadillac where she taught high school French for two years.

As soon as Green got his law degree, he enlisted in the Spanish-American War and commanded Company G, 31st Michigan Volunteer Infantry in Cuba. He came out a first lieutenant and when he returned he was appointed Assistant Inspector General of State Troops by Governor Hazen Pingree. (In 1899 he was promoted to Inspector General with the rank of Brigadier General.)

After the war, Green began practicing law in Ypsilanti. He was city attorney and became a partner in the Ypsilanti Reed Furniture Company. He and Helen were married on June 18, 1901. Within three years Green bought out his business associates and moved the company to Ionia.

The furniture company employed convicts in the Ionia prison at the suggestion of the warden and signed a contract for the work. The company grew to be the largest institution of its kind in the world. It used such vast quantities of reed that Green bought his own reed plantations in Malaya and had a branch office in Chicago.[2]

When Alex J. Groesbeck was state attorney general he attracted much public attention by investigations. One of these revealed prison labor being employed by private contractors. Green got out of his contract with the prison in 1923, but it is easy to see why he was no great friend of Groesbeck.

Green, meanwhile, was making money in many other businesses and banks. He was mayor of Ionia for 13 years, manager of the Ionia Free Fair, and treasurer of the State Central Republican Committee for 10 years. He had hundreds of friends throughout the state.

When Governor Groesbeck had completed his third term and was seeking nomination for a fourth term, many Republican party members wanted a change. They worked to secure the nomination for Green in the primary election and defeated the Groesbeck machine.

"With all the power Alex J. Groesbeck had accumulated in his three terms of oligarchical government…the people rose up and brought upon him the most tremendous political disaster that ever befell a political power in Michigan," Frank M. Sparks wrote in the Grand Rapids Herald, September 17, 1926.

Green went on to win the gubernatorial election by defeating Democrat William A. Comstock. He took office on a cold January 1st, 1927.

As governor, Green didn't forget his friends. James Oliver Curwood had helped him in his campaign because he wanted a conservationist governor. So Green had highway M-47 built from Owosso to Oakley. It went right by the clubhouse of the Shiawassee Conservation Club which Curwood had sponsored.[3]

Green wasn't concerned about any great reforms while he was governor, but he won major arguments with the legislature to increase workmen's compensation and to increase the gasoline tax from two to three cents a gallon. He also strengthened the conservation department and kept politics out of it.

He was elected for a second term and, when that was up, didn't seek re-election. He and Helen enjoyed their beautiful mansion on the bank of the Grand River where they had raised their daughter, Helen Nancy. Her daughter, Helen Tyrrell, lived with them.

Green was at his lodge "Camp Kennedy" near Munising in the Upper Peninsula when he died of peritonitis, on November 30, 1936. He was 64 years old.

Governor Wilber M. Brucker
1931 and 1932

By the time Wilber Brucker took office as governor, the depression was in full swing and he didn't get elected to a second term. "I went into office as a poor man and came out poorer," he remarked.[1] His career was far from over, however. Twenty-two years later he was appointed Secretary of the Army by President Dwight D. Eisenhower.

Wilber Marion was born at Saginaw, June 23, 1894, the third and youngest son of Ferdinand and Robertha Brucker. His father, a lawyer and a Democratic congressman, was defeated for re-election when Wilber was four and he died five years later.

"We were in pretty bad shape," Brucker recalled. "My father had been ill for six years and that sapped all the family fortune. We were left the home free and clear, but it was tough. An aunt, who taught school, came to live with us and that helped out."[2]

To do his share, young Brucker pulled mustard weeds out of corn fields at a penny a row. He had other part-time jobs until he graduated from Saginaw High School in 1912. Then he worked summers at a lumber yard in Saginaw and waited on table in Ann Arbor, to pay his way through law school at the University of Michigan.

He'd joined the National Guard while at the University and as soon as he graduated in 1916, he was mustered into service. He was sent to the Mexican border with the Michigan troops to put down Pancho Villa's raids. Within weeks after his regiment arrived back home, World War I was declared. Brucker was sent for officer training and was shipped out to France as a second lieutenant on September 13, 1917.

Brucker was assigned to the 42nd "Rainbow" Division and served in all its engagements in France. He was awarded a Silver Star for valor and a Purple Heart for wounds and came out of the war a first lieutenant.

Returning to Saginaw, Brucker began his law practice in a tiny, cubby-hole office. For eight years he and Clara Hantel had been sweethearts. She was the daughter of a Saginaw minister and had wanted to finish her education and have a career. She was working in the East but returned to Michigan and they were married on August 18, 1923.

Although his father had been a Democrat, Brucker's mother was a Republican and her influence was longest and strongest. The Republican congressman who had defeated his father was a friend of the family, however, and he took Wilber under his wing. Brucker became an active Republican party member. He was appointed and then elected Saginaw County Prosecutor. In 1927 he went to Lansing when he was appointed an assistant attorney general and the following year he was elected state attorney general.

In 1930, Brucker declared he was a candidate for governor and got the Republican nomination. He was just 36 when he won the election. He always said that his chief claim to fame was that he was the last Republican governor to hold office when Herbert Hoover was president. Hoover was his political idol and they were good friends for more than 20 years.[3]

"All during my administration we were fighting the depression," Brucker recalled. Banks were closing and 43 percent of the workingmen in Michigan cities were unemployed by 1932. Brucker cut his own salary by ten percent and reduced the number of state employees to make the government more economical.

He opposed state aid to jobless industrial workers. He had worked his own way through hard times and he believed the workers needed jobs, not handouts. He created relief jobs and launched a huge highway building program. He also had the legislature pass a road bill as a tax relief measure.

When he ran for re-election in 1932, Brucker was defeated by William Comstock who had run against him two years earlier. The only Republican in a state office to survive the national landslide by Franklin D. Roosevelt, was Frank D. Fitzgerald, the incumbent secretary of state.

Leaving Lansing with their son, Wilber II, Brucker joined a Detroit law firm from 1937 to 1954. He became very wealthy and they built a substantial home in Grosse Pointe Farms. Brucker had a flair for old-fashioned oratory and a politician's memory for names. He was five feet 10 inches tall and a non-smoking, non-drinking, church-going Presbyterian.

Brucker continued to work for the next twenty years within the Republican party on the state and national level. He ran for a U.S. Senate seat in 1936, but was defeated.

Things changed when Republican Dwight D. Eisenhower was elected President. He appointed Brucker general counsel of the Department of Defense in 1954 and Secretary of the Army in 1955, a post he held until 1961.

During this time their son carried on in the Detroit law firm and Brucker and Clara lived in Washington, D.C. They traveled a great deal and she took photographs and kept a diary which she later used for a book. They returned to their home in Michigan in 1961, when "Ike" left office and Brucker was no longer in the cabinet.

On October 28, 1968, 74 year-old Brucker was attending a meeting of the Economic Club in Detroit when he collapsed. He was taken to the Harper Hospital emergency room where he died of an apparent heart attack.

Ten years later, March 25, 1978, the United States Army Band building was named officially the Wilber M. Brucker Hall at Ft. Meyer, Virginia. It is located just 100 yards beyond the walls of Arlington National Cemetery where Brucker and Clara are buried.

Governor William A. Comstock
1933 and 1934

G etting to be governor of Michigan wasn't easy for William A.
Comstock. The Democrats had been on the outside of Michigan
government for 78 years and hadn't held a governorship in 16
years. When the party was on its last leg, Comstock came along. A
millionaire, he poured a lot of his own money into the Democratic party.
He let them put his name up for governor three times when no one else
would run because there wasn't a chance of winning. Comstock cared.

Then, after he finally won the 1932 election he didn't get the party's nomination for a second term. Comstock explained this action by saying, "The Democratic party of Michigan does not know how to act as a majority party." In his bitter farewell to the party in 1936, he referred to the Poles and Irish as "Hogski's and O'Piggy's," villains disrupting the party peace. Sometime later he denounced the Democratic party, Roosevelt, the New Deal and all its works... "[1]

Actually, Comstock was a gentleman and had a sense of humor. People always remembered his "pumphandle " laugh and cheerful personality. But when he wanted to, he could make some very pointed and blunt remarks like those above.

"Bill" as he liked to be called, was born in Alpena on July 2, 1877. His father, William B. Comstock was a lumber baron and young Bill rode the logs on Northern Michigan lumber rivers when he was a boy. He became an expert woodsman, went to the Alpena schools and worked for his father's electric railroad system. Then he went to the University of Michigan and graduated in 1899.

Considering the fact that he always looked like he'd been born in a suit with a white tie, it is surprising to learn that while at the University he was an amateur boxer and later boxed briefly as a professional in Chicago. He was a complex man and his life went up and down like a roller coaster.

In 1907 Comstock organized and became president of the State Savings Bank in Alpena. Then he took over the family fortune. He carried on the family lumber business, went into railroading in three states, became a banker, mine operator, newspaper publisher and plunged into the real estate business.[2]

Comstock began his political career as a Democrat county chairman in 1911 and two years later was elected mayor of the city of Alpena. In 1914 he was appointed to the Board of Regents of the University of Michigan by the Democrat Governor, Woodbridge Ferris.

During World War I, Comstock went to officers training school at Fort Sheridan in 1917, but after three months was discharged because of defective eyesight. He was active in civilian war work and the Red Cross. His life had again gone from up to down.

When he was a 41 year-old bachelor he met 38 year-old Josephine White Morrison, from a wealthy Detroit family, and they were married in 1919. He adopted her son by a previous marriage, changing his name to Kirke White Comstock. Little more than a year later they had a son, William Comstock III.

Comstock held the Democrat party together through the years the Republicans had almost complete control of local as well as state government. He ran for governor in 1926, 1928 and 1930. He contributed $250,000 of his own money to keep the party going. Several times he paid the expenses for delegates to go to the national Democrat conventions.

When the 1932 election came up, however, Comstock had lost his millions in the Great Depression. He was broke. He told the Democrats they'd have to raise money for his campaign if they wanted him to be a candidate for governor again. Franklin Roosevelt won the election by a landslide and this helped Comstock finally win a gubernatorial race— a high in his life.

After the 1929 stock market crash the depression had spread to Michigan. Voters looked to Roosevelt's New Deal to pull them out, but it only deepened during Comstock's two years in office.

Comstock did his best. He declared a bank holiday within six weeks of taking office. All financial institutions were closed for eight days in an effort to keep them from collapsing. With his banking experience, Comstock understood this was important to keep from having a disastrous run on all the banks. But his name was linked with financial problems from then on.

Under his administration prohibition was repealed, an emergency relief agency was set up, millions were spent on work projects, a sales tax was passed, an old-age pension system was approved, and other steps were taken to help people. But it wasn't enough for some of the Democrats who wanted more federal aid.

The party split into factions and Frank Murphy was a leader of those who wanted more New Deal projects. He was mayor of Detroit at the time. (Murphy was elected governor in 1936.) He became a friend of

Roosevelt and had more influence than Comstock, who was the governor.

Comstock told the press that "…there was no necessity for Frank to go down to New York and get into the Roosevelt organization through the back door. He could have come right through the front door with us." [4]

It was a losing battle for Comstock. He said he wouldn't campaign for re-election in 1934, he'd let his record stand for itself. Another Democrat, Arthus J. Lacy, announced that he was running for the nomination for governor to establish "Rooseveltian Democracy" in Michigan. Lacy won the nomination but lost the election in the fall to Republican Frank Fitzgerald.

A discouraged man, Comstock returned to Ann Arbor where he had been living. He'd lost millions in the depression and kept going cheerfully. But when his own party ditched him for New Deal leadership, it was as though his purpose in living was gone.

He started rebuilding his fortune in the real estate business and moved back to Detroit. When Frank Murphy ran for governor in 1936, Comstock understandably "took a walk" from the party. Later he ran for the Detroit City Council as a nonpartisan candidate and won easily. He also served on the Wayne County Board of Supervisors and was happy to be back in the political saddle. In later years he supported Harry Truman for president on the Democrat ticket.

After a series of three strokes over the years, however, Comstock was stricken again while at his hunting club near his hometown of Alpena. He was 71 when he died three weeks later in the Alpena hospital on June 16, 1949.

Governor Frank D. Fitzgerald
1935 and 1936
1939 for two and one-half months

When he was a boy, Frank Fitzgerald often accompanied his father from Grand Ledge to the Capitol building in Lansing. His father, John W. Fitzgerald had worked as a clerk of the House committee in one session and two years later was elected to the Michigan House of Representatives (1895-96). Young Fitzgerald grew up talking about good government and Republican politics at the dinner table and just naturally turned to a career in public service.[1]

Born January 27, 1885, Frank had an older sister and brother, Pearl and Harry. Their mother, Carrie, took care of the three children while their father ran a business in town. He later served in the Michigan legislature and then was the Grand Ledge postmaster the rest of his life.

Living in a small town on the Grand River gave Frank a good solid foundation. Everyone knew everyone and they all liked the Fitzgerald family. He loved horses and bought his own pony, paying for it by running a 10 cent delivery service. He left high school in the spring of his senior year to study business at Ferris Institute in Big Rapids. He was always sorry he didn't stay to graduate.

While taking classes at Ferris he spent two summers in the west, working on farms and ranches. About this time he also decided to change his middle name, Thaddeus, to Dwight. From then on he was known as Frank D.

Returning to Grand Ledge, his father hired him to work as a clerk in the post office and he held the job for about five years. During this time Queena Maud Warner moved from Mulliken, a nearby farming community, to be the secretary for the owner of the Grand Ledge Chair Company. She, too, had been a student at Ferris Institute, although they didn't know each other there, and the couple was married on June 28, 1909.

In 1912, when Frank was 27, he made his first political move. He ran for the Eaton County Board of Supervisors against a Democrat incumbent and campaigned hard. When he won, he was the first Republican and the youngest member to serve on the board.

Fitzgerald had found his calling. He liked the political scene and he was eager to go to Lansing where the action was. The logical step was to get a job at the Capitol and in 1913 he was hired as a committee clerk in the state senate. Two years later, in 1915, he became a proof reader in the house of representatives and two years after that, in 1917, he became a bill clerk in the House. Legislative sessions in those days were held only the first three months or less, of each the year, and Fitzgerald had a wife to support. He filled in the rest of the months as a clerk in the Secretary of State's office. During these years he learned how state government worked from the inside.

When World War I started, Fitzgerald was 32 and the Federal Food Administration asked him to be executive secretary of the Michigan Food Administration. He took on the job until it was completed in 1919.

About this time the new secretary of state appointed him deputy secretary of state. By now the Fitzgeralds were living in Lansing and his career in government was progressing well. But in 1920 he entered the business world as an officer in an Oldsmobile dealership in Tennessee. The Fitzgeralds moved to Memphis. But this didn't work out. People liked the cars but they couldn't drive them without good roads.

The Fitzgeralds returned to Grand Ledge in 1923 and it was here that their only child, John Warner, was born on November 14, 1924.

Soon after their return to Michigan, Governor Alex J. Groesbeck appointed Fitzgerald business manager of the State Highway Department and he worked there for seven years. After his venture into the business world, he was glad to be back in the Capitol.

He did a good job as manager during the golden era of road-building. He also was thinking like a good politician. When new highways or bridges were built, he would be on hand for the opening ceremonies. He spoke to groups all around the state about the operation of the highway department and met thousands of people this way. He made friends and they remembered him.

Fitzgerald was six feet tall, weighed 180 pounds and was a bundle of energy. He wore plain clothes, dark gray suits and plain black ties... always well dressed. In the winter his black overcoat, white scarf and black derby were almost uniforms. He made time for his son and preferred hiking with him to playing golf in the summers.

Although he was mentioned as a candidate for governor early on, his political instincts told him to start with the office of Secretary of State. He was elected in 1930 and made still more friends. Again in 1932, he was urged to run for governor, but instead he ran for a second term as

Secretary of State and won. He was the only Republican elected when the Democrats swept the election and put Governor Comstock in office.

In 1934, the Democrats were split. Fitzgerald ran for governor and won. His term was noted for fiscal responsiblity and a balanced state budget, a remarkable feat during the lingering depression. But 1936 was a presidential election year and President Franklin Roosevelt's popularity carried Frank Murphy into the Michigan governorship.

Two years later, when it wasn't a presidential race, Fitzgerald entered the campaign and defeated Murphy. He worked so hard to regain the governor's seat, however, that he practically ruined his health. Within 10 weeks after taking office for his second term, he fell ill with what was diagnosed as influenza and exhaustion from overwork. His heart had been damaged and four days later he died on March 16, 1939, at the age of 54.

Fitzgerald was the only governor to die while in office. Ten thousand people paid tribute to him at the Capitol and eight thousand lined the streets of Grand Ledge at his funeral. His popularity has puzzled many political observers, but at least part of it was due to his philosophy, "Never forget a friend. Make new ones if you can, but never sacrifice an old one for a new."

Governor Frank Murphy
1937 and 1938

Before and after Frank Murphy was governor, he had many political friends and enemies. But his political friend in the White House is the one that charted his life. President Franklin Roosevelt appointed Murphy to more high offices in national government than any other former Michigan governor has held.

Frank Murphy's father, John, had worked his way through the University of Michigan Law School and settled at Sand Beach in the 1880s to practice law. Frank's mother, Mary Brennan, was a country schoolteacher. They were Irish, Catholic and Democrats. They bought a building for his law office and lived in the rooms behind it.

The Murphy's four children were born in the home behind the office. Harold was the oldest, then Frank and George. They had one sister, Marguerite. Actually, Frank was baptized William Francis, but he never used his first name and this left him without a middle initial. He was born on April 13, 1890, but decided later in his career that he had been born in 1893, so records vary.

Frank's boyhood was a happy one and he always cherished the peace and quiet of a small town. The family moved into a large house two doors south of the law office and he went to the public school in Harbor Beach. He was a good student, a quarterback on the high school football team, played on the baseball team, was on the track team and an excellent debater. When he graduated from high school his mother gave him a Bible inscribed with "To Dear Frank from Mamma on the day he graduated, June 26, 1908."

Although his mother had died by the time he was sworn in as U.S. Attorney General, Murphy had the Bible with him and President Roosevelt autographed it. He used it on other swearing-in ceremonies too.[1]

Following his high school graduation, Murphy entered the University of Michigan and worked summers for the Huron Milling Company for $1.75 a day. When he got his degree in law he joined a firm in Detroit until the United States entered World War I. He enlisted and served overseas, becoming a captain in the infantry.

Just three days after his discharge, Murphy was sworn in as first assistant U. S. attorney for the Eastern District of Michigan. He resigned from the post in March 1922 and went into private law practice, Murphy and Kemp, with his closest friend. A year later he became a winning candidate for a seat on Detroit's Recorder's Court and served for six years.[2]

Murphy had red hair and was a bachelor. Women chased him, but he put his career first and never married. He didn't smoke nor drink and was a devout Catholic. He attended mass regularly and daily read the Bible his mother had given him. He was also keenly interested in politics and, although he spoke softly, he hit hard when he thought it was necessary. He looked upon his work in public office as a kind of ministry.

Murphy was a complex character. He was an egotistical man and a compassionate man. He was soft-hearted and sentimental but relished a good fight with an opponent. He enjoyed being with the rich and famous, but he never forgot the poor and downtrodden. He wanted organization in government but was known as an untidy administrator. He was a staunch Democrat but appointed Republicans to offices if he thought they were the most capable.

When the mayor of Detroit was recalled by the voters in July 1930, Murphy entered the race and won it. He was re-elected the next year. But by now Detroit was in the middle of the depression that left about 50,000 people out of jobs and destitute. Murphy did everything he could to give relief to those in need. He was a New Dealer before Roosevelt's New Deal and he campaigned hard for Roosevelt thoughout the state. The two became good friends.

This was when Governor Comstock, another Democrat, was in office. A faction of the party wanted more public welfare programs than Comstock could get the legislature to pass. The fight got so hot among Democrats that the Republicans won the next gubernatorial election with Frank Fitzgerald (1934).

Appreciating Murphy's support, President Roosevelt appointed him governor-general of the Philippines and after being there for two years he was named the U.S. High Commissioner. His sister, Marguerite Murphy Teahan and her husband went with him to the Philippines and from that time on she served as Murphy's hostess wherever he went.[3]

Roosevelt thought he needed Murphy on the ticket to carry Michigan in the 1936 election, however, and had him return from the Philippines for the campaign. It turned out the other way around. Roosevelt's popularity pulled Murphy along with him into the governor's office.

In the two years he was governor, Murphy brought a Little New Deal to the state and improved the administrative structure. He got into hot water, though, when he wouldn't use troops in breaking a sit-down strike at the General Motors plant in Flint. At first his negotiations that brought a peaceful settlement between the labor union and management were praised. But then the sit-down strikes spread and Murphy got the blame.

When the next (1938) election came up, it wasn't tied in with a presidential election and the state voters put former Republican Governor Fitzgerald back in office. Murphy was also not a strict party man and the Democrats weren't well organized.

Soon after Murphy's defeat for re-election as governor, President Roosevelt called him to the White House and appointed him Attorney General of the United States. He went to Washington in 1939 and tackled the job so hard that many political scandals were exposed. Some labor union leaders were even glad when Roosevelt moved him out of this office by appointing him to the U. S. Supreme Court in 1940. He became Michigan's only Supreme Court Justice.

Through the years Murphy guided G. Mennen Williams along the path to becoming governor of Michigan. He helped him get jobs and gave him lots of advice.

Murphy liked to return to Harbor Beach for summer vacations and in July 1949, he hadn't been feeling well so stopped in Detroit's Henry Ford Hospital for a checkup. During the few days he was there his condition wasn't considered serious but on July 19, he died of a heart attack. He was just 59 years old.

Twenty thousand persons passed by his casket in Detroit's City Hall and an equal number were turned away. Murphy was buried in the cemetery at Harbor Beach along with other family members. They all have plain cedar cross markers on their graves and his reads: Frank Murphy, Justice Supreme Court.

Note: The house where Frank Murphy was born in Harbor Beach has been turned into a museum and is operated by the Huron County Historical Society.

Governor Luren D. Dickinson
1939 and 1940

Luren Dudley Dickinson was sick with influenza in his farm home in Eaton County when word came that Governor Frank Fitzgerald had died. Only 10 weeks earlier, Fitzgerald had retaken the office he'd held in 1935-36 but lost to Frank Murphy. Now Fitzgerald was dead and, because he was lieutenant governor, Dickinson was sworn in as governor.

Ironically, during the recent campaign Republican Fitzgerald had caused a furor by saying, as a joke, the Democrat running for Lt. Governor would probably become governor if he died while in office. But it happened and rather than a Democrat, it was the 79 year-old Republican who became governor.

This was one of the rare mistakes Fitzgerald ever made as a politician. Lieutenant governors were elected on their own then and it wasn't until the 1963 Constitution was adopted that the governor and lieutenant governor were elected as a team. Like many others, Fitzgerald had underestimated the old farmer. When the votes were counted, Dickinson was elected with the largest majority of anyone on the Republican ticket.

Dickinson had been elected lieutenant governor seven times on his own. In his first race, 1914, he'd won the seat when Democrat Woodbridge Ferris was re-elected governor and continued in the office when Republican Albert Sleeper was governor. Six years later he won elections three more times, serving under Governors Fred Green and Wilber Brucker. It wasn't until 1939 that he was elected again as Lt. Governor for Governor Fitzgerald.

When Fitzgerald died on March 16, 1939, the question was raised by some as to whether Dickinson would become governor or serve as acting governor until a new governor was elected or appointed. Precedent had been set in the mid-1800s, for the lieutenant governor to fill out a term as acting governor when the governor resigned to take another job in Washington.

There was no question in Dickinson's mind. He got out of bed, came downstairs and the Eaton County Clerk administered the oath of office to him as governor at 8:20 a.m., on March 17, the day after Fitzgerald had died. That settled it. At 79, he was the oldest person to ever become Governor of Michigan. His first act was to ask his pastor of the Charlotte Methodist Church to say a prayer.[1]

What made Dickinson such a vote getter was a puzzlement to other politicians. In one election, although he was a "dry", Wayne County which was "wet", gave him a majority vote.

Some things he wrote about himself help explain this.[2]

"I was born in Niagara County, New York, on April 12, 1859. My parents brought me to Michigan a year later and after moving around for four years, settled on part of the farm that I now own, there being 30 acres in the farm at that time. (He added acreage until it was a 250-acre farm.)

"My parents faced the problem of building a home, paying a mortgage and raising three chilldren; a sister, a brother and myself.

"They started me to school in the country when I was four. I averaged six months in the year until I was 12 and was taken out to help my father on the farm."

As Dickinson grew older, despite his parents objections, he went with his friends "to card parties, dances and hung around the pool-rooms and saloons." But he wanted an education and saved his money by raising odd crops or working for a neighbor to pay his tuition and buy his books. He went without dinners to save money. He walked three miles to school and back, studying at home mights so he could get a job teaching.

"In a little more than two years I put in two summers' work on the farm, taught two terms of school and took a large part of the four years course in high school," he recalled. During the first term of teaching little children he realized he should set a good example for them, he said, and this changed his life. He would have liked to have become a lawyer and studied for the bar exam, but didn't pass it because he lacked practical experience. So he continued to teach school and work on the farm "until middle life," as he put it.

When Dickinson was 21 he was elected Superintendent of Schools and began his lifelong work in the Republican party. When he was 24 he joined the neighborhood church and was active in it, too, for the rest of his life.

In his first term of teaching, Zora Della Cooley was a student of his. She was a soloist and organist in the church and he had never heard anyone sing like she did. It wasn't long before 24 year-old Luren and 18 year-old Zora were married on October 16, 1888.

The newlyweds moved in with his parents and lived with them from then on. "It isn't always advisable for young married people to do this," he wrote later, "But we found very little that was disagreeable…and worked together nicely." They were also able to " lay up" something this way, a habit he'd formed early in his teaching career. They had no children but they adopted a niece, Rilla Ethel. Her brother, Verl Vinton, lived with them for several years, too.

After being elected to local and township offices, Dickinson was urged to run for county clerk and was told he'd get the nomination easily. When he didn't get it, he learned an important lesson. "I investigated and found that there are two ways of expressing ones' self," he said. He preferred to look at it that way than to think some of the other delegates had lied.

He was elected to the legislature in 1896 and served two years. Although nominated for another term, he withdrew when asked to write a statement that wasn't true. "I informed these leaders that I would take orders from no one other than the electorate and drew out of the campaign." It was six years before he was re-elected to the House for two terms. (1905-6 and 1907-8). He worked hard to get a primary election law passed. Following this, he went to the state senate for two years.

During this time Dickinson became increasingly involved in the Anti-Saloon League and traveled as its president around the state speaking for a law which would give counties the right to hold elections to make the selling of liquor illegal. People supporting this were called "Dry" and those that opposed it were called "Wet." Dickinson was as dry as you could get.

He was also a vice-president in the Woman's Suffrage campaign and was outspoken against gambling and other "sins."

In 1910 Dickinson was defeated for the party nomination to run for lieutenant governor but four years later he was elected to the post. Although lieutenant governors didn't give inaugural addresses, he startled the state by giving one, expressing his opinions on prohibition. He always dressed formally, wearing wing collars, cut-away coats, striped trousers and black, high laced shoes. Some of the younger legislators said they liked to shake his hand so they could hear the cuffs rattle on his starched shirts.

He always drove the 20 miles from Charlotte to Lansing, to be in his office early each morning. He never did any business on Sundays. He taught Sunday School and went to Church. Always careful with money, he once sent a post card to his office while on a trip, saying the legislators should talk less and pray more... and made a note at the end with an important government decision.

Other politicians may have poked fun at Dickinson, but he was the one who raked in the votes and won elections. By the time the 1938 election rolled around, Dickinson was urged to run for lieutenant governor again although he didn't think he had a chance for the nomination. Fitzgerald had suggested the incumbent shouldn't have competition for the office, they were both from Eaton County and his crusade as a "Dry" might keep some Republicans from supporting him.[3]

However, he let his friends get a petition out and he won the nomination. Everyone, including Dickinson was surprised. Then, even more surprising, he won the election as lieutenant governor and, when Fitzgerald died, became governor.

During his nearly two years in office he called out the State Police in a statewide drive against slot machines. He took issue with groups that opposed his ideas, such as the friends of civil service. A law was passed requiring teachers to take an oath of allegiance to the government.

Although he was popular with the people and tried to carry out the promises Fitzgerald had made, special interests were unhappy with him. Plans were announced to circulate petitions for his recall, for "conduct unbecoming the chief executive of Michigan."[4]

Dickinson got a charge out of it. He offered to sign a petition saying, "I never wanted to be governor." This made everyone laugh and the movement collapsed. He also went to New York to a governor's conference where he saw the "high life" as he called it. He came back and preached one of his sermons on the radio about the moral looseness in the big city.

A sad note was when his wife, Zora, who had been ill most of the time he was governor, died about five months before his term ended.

Since he became governor there hadn't been a lieutenant governor and Dickinson appointed Matilda Dodge Wilson to fill the vacancy in mid-November. This caused an uproar. Considering his age some politicians were terrified lest the state would end up with a woman governor. But she served the last few weeks during his term and they both went out of office the next January.

Of course Dickinson didn't just fade out. He ran for re-election in 1940. He was 81 and he hired a 61 year-old to run his campaign, so some called it the youth movement. This election he lost, however, to Democrat Murray D. Van Wagoner and returned to his farm. Two years later he considered running against Van Wagoner, but reluctantly gave up the idea. He died on April 22, 1943 at the age of 84 and was buried beside Zora in the Charlotte cemetery.

Governor Murray D. Van Wagoner
1941 and 1942

W hen Murray D. Van Wagoner had been governor for not quite a year, the Japanese bombed Pearl Harbor in Hawaii and World War II was declared. He led the way for Michigan to become the "Arsenal of Democracy, with nearly all of its 6,000 factories working on defense contracts.

Van Wagoner's forefathers came to New York from Holland and his great-grandfather came to Michigan in 1820. His father James, and his mother, Florence Lomis, were farming in the Thumb, near Kingston, when he was born on March 18, 1898. It was just five minutes after St. Patrick's Day, so the Doctor said he'd call the baby "Pat"... and they could name him what they wanted later. They named him Murray Delos, but "Pat" stuck and the Dutch boy grew up with an Irish nickname.

He had one brother, Jacob, who grew up to own an insurance agency in Pontiac and one sister, Esther Van Wagoner Tufty, who became a nationally known journalist.

The family moved to Pontiac when Pat was three years old and his father was a life insurance agent there from 1902 until his death. The Van Wagoner kids kept busy when they weren't in school. Pat and his brother delivered papers for the *Pontiac Press* and on Saturdays they picked up empty wooden pails on doorsteps to return to a creamery to make some extra money.[1]

While in Pontiac High School, Pat played tackle on the football team and played in the orchestra. Although he'd been pals with Helen Josephine Jossman in grade school now they became sweethearts. The only dates they ever had were with each other.

After graduating from high school in 1917, Van Wagoner worked his way through the University of Michigan's Engineering school. In addition to working nights in Marquardt's Garage, he played center on the football team until he was sidelined by a knee injury as a sophomore. He was vice president of his senior class when he graduated with a B.S. degree in Civil Engineering in 1921.

Pat began his career as a project engineer for the Michigan State Highway Department that same year. The headquarters for his district were in Alpena, so he borrowed Helen's Model A Ford for his surveying work. Within three years he joined an engineering firm in Pontiac and he and Helen were married on June 7, 1924.

During the next six years Van Wagoner started his own engineering firm and got into local politics. Although his family was Republican, he had to run as a Democrat to get on a ballot. He lost on his bid for the Oakland County Surveyors office in 1928. But in 1930, "they stuck my name on the ballot without asking me, and I was elected (county) drain commissioner," he recalled later. He was re-elected for a second term.

By July 1, 1933, Van Wagoner was Michigan's new state highway commissioner and moved to Lansing with Helen and their two toddlers, Ellen Louise and Jo Ann. He took over the job with gusto, directing the greatest road building program in Michigan history.

He was re-elected to another four-year term and was responsible for the first roadside park along a state highway system and established the nation's first permanent travel information center at New Buffalo. Every time he heard of a natural spring along a highway, he'd try to purchase surrounding land so it could be used for one of the parks.

The Van Wagoner name became well known thoughout the state and he ended up with a political machine of his own. He was described as "big, breezy, boisterous with a broad, beaming smile and laughter that shouts. He likes cigars, children, dogs, games and simple ways of living. 'Pat' works hard and plays hard all the time. He's a hearty man, likes having people around him and loves the strenuous life."[2]

In 1940 the Democrats insisted Van Wagoner run for governor and the Republicans nominated 81 year-old Governor Dickinson as their candidate. The friendly Democrat with a ready handshake won the election.

A 5-foot, 9-inch man who weighed about 200 pounds, Van Wagoner wasn't a good public speaker. He often bungled the speech he was reading and blurted out remarks that aides would try to keep from getting into newspapers. He was later tutored and became a competent after-dinner orator.[3]

Although he had projects he hoped to undertake, World War II took precedence and Van Wagoner devoted most of his time to the war effort. He launched the civilian defense program and organized the home guard. He also had to see that strikes didn't interrupt the production of essential war materials and he succeeded.

Years later when he filled out a biographical information sheet for the State Library, Van Wagoner wrote a summary of posts he'd held. As State Highway Commissioner he wrote he was in "charge of all State Roads" and as Governor of Michigan he was in "charge of all People". Friends agreed that he liked the highway job the best.

Although he ran for re-election in 1942, Van Wagoner was defeated by Republican Harry Kelly and returned to private business. In 1946 he was convinced to make another try for governor but was defeated again, this time by Kim Sigler. President Harry Truman then apppointed him U. S. military governor of Bavaria in October 1947, and he was there for two years.

The Van Wagoners liked it in Bavaria, the bread basket of Germany. But the pay was low and they returned in two years. He brought back mounted trophies from his boar hunting expeditions and they still hang in the Detroit Club. By 1950 he was in a private firm as a consulting engineer in Detroit and the family lived in a large, rambling house in Birmingham. He came back, he said, "To make some money for the family and myself.

At last he had time to camp in the north woods during deer season, play golf, go bowling and play bridge or poker. One of his favorite hobbies was photography, including home movies. The entire family liked to play dominoes and were all very good at it, too.

The couple had been married for almost 62 years when Helen died in 1986. Van Wagoner died just seven weeks later, on June 12th at the age of 88.

Governor Harry F. Kelly
1943 through 1946

Harry F. Kelly, a big friendly Irishman, was a hero in World War I and was known as Michigan's War Governor in World War II.

Actually, Governor Van Wagoner was in office during the first year of the war which began on December 7, 1941, and he laid the groundwork for the wartime years ahead. But he didn't win re-election in 1942. Republican Kelly took over where Van Wagoner left off and his two terms carried him through the war and into peacetime.

Harry Francis Kelly and a twin sister were born on April 19, 1895, the first of Henry and Molly Morrisey Kelly's five sons and four daughters. They were all born in Ottawa, Illinois, where their father was an attorney. Their mother's father, Larry Morrisey, was a Republican whip in the Illinois legislature.

His grandfather Morrisey had a great influence on young Harry. He'd take him out of classes for baseball games, political party barbecues and other political functions. When the family complained, his grandfather would tell them, "Shucks, there's a lot of things a boy can't learn in school."[1]

Harry loved to play baseball and other sports as he grew up and graduated from high school. He wanted to become a lawyer but his father kept him out of college for a year to spend time in court with him and so he could see the practical side of the profession. "There are a lot of things about the law you can't get out of Blackstone. A good lawyer's life is a lot of sweat," he told his son.

When the year was up, Kelly enrolled in the University of Notre Dame and was completing his studies in law school there when the United States declared war against Germany on April 6, 1917. He enlisted that same day but was granted leave from Camp Sheridan in June to return to Notre Dame and receive his degree.

Kelly was sent to France as a second lieutenant with the 9th Infantry, Second Division of the United States Army. He was wounded and received the Croix de Guerre, with Palm. (With Palm means with an emblem of victory). His citation reads, "Wounded in two legs and made prisoner by five Germans, this Officer valiantly defended himself and escaped with the help of some men who came to his aid. Wounded a second time, he passed the entire night at the bottom of a trench before being able to be evacuated."

As a result of his wounds, Kelly lost his right leg and seldom knew a day free of pain the rest of his life. But he didn't let this keep him from his ambition to practice law or get into politics. Shortly after returning home to Illinois in 1919, he was elected state's attorney for LaSalle County for a four year term.

Meanwhile, since four of the five Kelly boys had become lawyers, his father decided there wasn't enough legal business in the town of Ottawa for so many Kellys. He moved to Detroit in 1922 and started a law firm, Kelly and Kelly, with his son Emmett. Harry joined them three years later. [2]

It wasn't long before Harry met Anne O'Brien at a bridge party given by her sister. Anne was a physical education teacher who had come to Detroit when she was a 5 year-old from the Upper Peninsula. Her father had an insurance company in Detroit. Her Uncle was a well known judge in the U.P. who had moved to Detroit and was a Wayne County judge.

The O'Briens were strong liberal Democrats and quite upset when a year later Anne married Republican Harry Kelly on May 4, 1929. Within a few years they had six children: Joanne, twins Harry F., Jr. and Brian J., Lawrence, Roger and Mary. Visitors compared their happy, active, household to a railroad station in a big city.

While Anne was bearing and raising their children, Kelly was becoming more and more involved in politics. He was appointed assistant prosecuting attorney in Wayne County in 1930, named manager of the Detroit office of the Michigan Liquor Control Commission in 1935, elected secretary of state in 1938 and re-elected in 1940.

By this time he was so popular with voters that the Republicans convinced him to run for governor in 1942. There was no presidential race this year and Kelly defeated Governor Van Wagoner to win the election.

Much of his first two years in office were spent in seeing that the machinery was kept running to make Michigan the arsenal of democracy. He did all he could to make the state a leader in the war effort. This kept him from making all of the improvements he wanted to make on the home front, but he managed to make several of them.

One of his major problems was the 1943 race riot in Detroit. He finally had to declare martial law get federal troops to put down the riot and restore peace.

In 1944 he ran for re-election and for the first time in 14 years an incumbent succeeded himself in office. During this time it had been an in-and out-series of governors. And, for the first time since 1928 a Republican won as governor of Michigan in a presidential election year.

Kelly is probably best remembered for getting a Veteran's Trust Fund set up which helped soldiers returning from the war get back on their feet. When he left office there was $51 million in the fund and a surplus in the state treasury.

After two terms as governor, Kelly retired and returned to private law practice in Detroit. He'd wanted more time with his family and now he could enjoy being with them in their log cabin home on a lake near Gaylord. He was a man of simple tastes who was most comfortable in khaki slacks and flannel shirts.[3]

Republicans called him back in 1950 to run against governor G. Mennen Williams and it was a real cliff-hanger. When the votes were first counted, Kelly had a majority. Then the official tally showed Williams was ahead. The Republicans demanded a recount and it was a month after the balloting before Williams was declared the winner by 1,154 votes.[4]

Three years later Kelly was elected to the State Supreme Court for an eight year term and re-elected in 1961. He throughly enjoyed these 16 years and of 480 opinions he offered, 300 were adopted as the unanimous views of the court.

Kelly retired on January 1, 1971, when he reached the mandatory retirement age. Just six weeks later on February 8, he suffered a massive stroke while in West Palm Beach, Florida, and died at the age of 75.

Governor Kim Sigler
1947 and 1948

This governor came riding into office like John Wayne or the Lone Ranger. Kim Sigler was born on a ranch out west but didn't grow up to ride herd on cattle rustlers. He came to Michigan and sent more than 50 big-scale grafters to jail and cleaned up the state legislature.

He was born Kimber Cornellus Zeigler on his father's 3,000-acre cattle ranch in Schuyler, Nebraska, on May 2, 1894. His father, Daniel, and mother, Bertha Zeigler had two children, Kim and his younger sister, Goldie. Later, in World War I, people with German names were often suspected of being anti-American and the Zeiglers changed their name to Sigler.

Kimber became Kim, he explained, because he liked the novel "Kim" by Rudyard Kipling, and he'd quote: "So live each day that you can look any man in the eye and tell him to go to hell." He not only adopted the name but tried to live up to those words throughout his life. Sometimes this backfired, but the newspapers loved it and so did their readers.

When he was seven, Kim was riding horses and by the time he was a teenager, he was roping, throwing and branding steers. He had chores to do in the morning before breakfast and in his spare time he worked out in a home-made boxing ring with his father. A veterinarian who was fair but tough, his father wanted Kim to be a rancher when he grew up. His mother wanted him to be a doctor or a lawyer.

In Gothenburg high school Kim played halfback and tackle on the football team. He was a catcher on the baseball team and played a little basketball but said, "I could never keep the football out of it." He also was on the debate team and was such a good speaker that his coach urged him to become a lawyer.

But first, he tried his hand at his favorite sport of boxing. He had 50 fights as an amateur and scored 20 knockouts. In the process he got his nose broken and lived with a rugged profile the rest of his life. He also took his father's advice to see the country and traveled across country as a hobo.

After graduating from high school in 1913, Kim arrived in Ann Arbor with $40 his mother had sewed into his vest pocket as a reserve fund against the "slickers back East." He enrolled in the University of Michigan and worked as a waiter at the University Hospital during two years of pre-law courses.[1]

It was while at the U of M that he met Mae Pierson, a student nurse from Goodrich, a small town southeast of Flint. The canoe she and a friend were paddling capsized on the Huron River and she couldn't swim. Sigler rescued her and after she graduated with her Registered Nurse degree, they were married.

Meanwhile, Sigler entered law school at the University of Detroit where he could work nights in the Highland Park plant of the Ford Motor Company and go to school days. He graduated in 1918, and worked for several different law offices in Detroit. In August the following year the couple had a baby girl named Betty, and they started looking for a small city where he could start his own practice.

The Siglers found their ideal place in Hastings, moved there in 1922 and made it their home for nearly a quarter of a century. Kim was likeable, easy to know and so ambitious that townsfolk must have felt at times like they had a tiger by the tail. He was elected Barry County prosecuting attorney on the Democrat ticket and was re-elected two times.

They had a beautiful home on Green Street and two more daughters were born to them, Beverly in 1923 and Goldie Madalon, four years later. Beverly died when she was eleven years old from infantile paralysis.

Sigler's office was so elegantly furnished that people came just to look at the place. He was active in the 151st Rotary International and, as district governor, he represented the organization in Nice, France. Meanwhile his reputation as a trial lawyer spread. He was colorful and spectacular in the courtroom and soon was trying cases in practically every circuit in the western part of Michigan.

In 1943 he formed a partnership with another lawyer in Battle Creek, but later that year he was asked to help clean up graft and corruption as a special prosecutor of the Ingham County grand jury. He was successful in obtaining 41 convictions and 11 pleas of guilty. Now the state courts began to think they had a tiger by the tail and politicians were sure of it.

Although a senate committee tried to slow Sigler down by saying his investigations were costing too much, he kept at it until they dismissed him from his job as special prosecutor. They overlooked the fact that he had gained a tremendous following among the voters in the state. He'd had wide publicity in his battles against corrupt government officials and letters and telegrams poured in urging him to run for governor.

Sigler had no political machine behind him but he had a well-known record. He had won the respect and admiration of the people. They loved his showmanship, his personality, his drive and his fighting spirit.

By 1946, when he ran for governor on the Republican ticket, Sigler was a handsome man with a strong face topped by gray hair streaked with white. He was five feet-ten inches tall, weighed 150 pounds and dressed fit-to-kill. He said his clothes were made by a tailoring establishment in Grand Rapids in payment for $3,000 in legal fees they owed him.

Estimates ranged from 45 to 73 suits hanging in his closet. He wore a broad-brimmed Western hat and soft doeskin gloves that became his trademark. His favorite cashmere topcoat, trimmed with purple piping and sporting a velvet collar, would have aroused pangs of jealousy in the breast of a Mississippi riverboat gambler.[2]

To the surprise of the regulars in the Republican party, Sigler won the election by 360,000 votes more than Democrat Murray D. Van Wagoner. But then he had to work with the legislators, some having felt the sting of his investigations, and they balked at all his proposals. He did establish a Department of Administration in an effort to reduce the number of boards and commissions which he said ran the government.

He strengthened the State Police and cleaned out the prison system. Some voters thought it was a wonder he accomplished as much as he did during his two years in office. In doing this, though, he made a lot of enemies.

Just before he took office as governor, Sigler learned to fly and it became his passion. He flew his own plane to meetings all over the state and during his campaign for re-election. He came under considerable criticism because he spent so much time flying rather than running things in the executive office.

There were other problems not as easily seen. For one thing, Sigler had promised more than he could deliver as governor. Perhaps the people had idolized him to the point that they expected far too much. And, many old guard Republicans sat on their hands in the next election.

Sigler lost to Democrat G. Mennen Williams in the 1948 election. He slipped out the back door of the Capitol during William's inauguration on January 1st, and rode to the airport alone. He picked up a sack at the lunch counter, headed for his plane and flew off with no regrets. "In another two years another guy will come along and he (Williams) won't be there any more. Only the history students and a few shabby politicians ever will know whether Kim Sigler served one term or two," he said.

He had made three mistakes. His first mistake was appointing Williams to the Liquor Control Board where he could build a base of voters. His second mistake was thinking Williams would only serve two years as governor. His third was assuming he wouldn't be remembered. He is still talked about in terms such as being publicity-wise, colorful, illustrious and fabulous. It is said that he lived and dressed dangerously and that he had the look of a pilot in his eyes.

The Siglers continued to live in Lansing, he entered a law firm and kept on flying. He flew from Lansing to the southern tip of Chile, all across the American continent and past the rim of the Arctic circle in his plane.[3]

He had a few minor mishaps, but always escaped injury until a freezing night on November 30, 1953. Sigler's plane crashed near Battle Creek when it clipped a TV broadcasting tower. He was 59 years old and died in as spectacular way as he had lived, in a blazing crash.

Perhaps it was a premonition. But Sigler liked his portrait which hangs under the capitol dome. In the background is his little red-and-silver airplane parked on the lawn in front of Michigan's capitol building.

Governor G. Mennen Williams
1949 through 1960

From the time he was young, Gerhard Mennen Williams liked to square dance. When he was older, he liked to call square dances and "called" his way through political campaigns, cranky legislatures and even meetings with foreign dignitaries.

He could also recall people's names when he'd met them only briefly. This was a big help in getting votes when he needed them later on.

G. Mennen was born into a wealthy family in Detroit on February 23, 1911. He had two younger brothers, Henry, Jr., who was born August 23, 1912, and Richard, who was 10 years younger. His father, Henry Phillips Williams, was the son of a well-to-do Detroit family. His mother, Elma Mennen, was the daughter of Gerhard Mennen who had made a fortune in toiletries. He had started in a tiny drugstore in New Jersey and founded the Mennen line of shaving lotions which are still found in bathroom cabinets all over the country.

It was only natural that his grandson and namesake would be called "Soapy," and the nickname stuck with Mennen through life. Henry was called "Lather" and Dick was "Suds," but they got rid of their nicknames.[1] The boys all went to church regularly and Soapy was very religious all his life.

Their parents loved to travel and took the boys with them on many trips. Other times, usually several months each year, his mother and father traveled and an aunt and uncle stayed with the boys. Another uncle took them hunting and fishing up north and Soapy loved this.

Young Mennen went to the Liggett Grade School in Detroit and to the Detroit University Grade School until he was 14. Then he was sent to the Salisbury School in Connecticut. He played on the football team, played basketball, baseball, track and was a member of the Athletic Committee. He also did very well in his studies. He especially liked Sundays when everyone wore tuxedoes and the students gave speeches in the auditorium.

It was while he was a sophomore at Salisbury that Williams decided to make public service his career so he could "help the underdogs" in society. When he graduated, he went to Princeton and made his first political move. He ran for and won the election to become president of the Young Republicans Club. This, too, was only natural because he came from a Republican family. About that time he also decided to be governor of Michigan one day.

After graduating from Princeton in 1933, Soapy entered law school at the University of Michigan and it was here that he decided to be a Democrat rather than a Republican. While at the U of M, he met Nancy Lace Quirk, a student in the School of Social Work. Nancy's father was a successful businessman in Ypsilanti and her older brother was mayor of the town.

A year after they met, Williams graduated from law school. The next year Nancy graduated and they were married a few weeks later on June 26, 1937. From then on the couple was a team in the Democrat party. They moved to Washington, D.C., where he held several federal government positions. Governor Frank Murphy, who had been an attorney for Williams parents, knew Soapy was interested in politics and took him under his wing.

When World War II was declared, Nancy returned to Ypsilanti and Williams began a four year stint with the United States navy. He earned ten battle stars in the Pacific theater and came home as a Lieutenant Commander in 1946.

Williams began working in Detroit as deputy directory of the Office of Price Administration (OPA) and in 1947 Governor Kim Sigler appointed him to the Liquor Control Commission. Meanwhile, they had their third child, Wendy. Gerhard "Gery" Mennen, Jr. had been born while they were in Washington and Nancy Quirk was born while her father was in the service.

In 1948 Soapy thought the time was right to get into race for the governorship. The Republicans were split, the Democrat party was weak and labor leaders were so disgusted with both organizations that they were thinking of forming their own party. Thousands of veterans were home from the war and could vote, ethnic groups in Detroit knew Soapy and conservationists thought they'd found a friend in him.

By bringing all these forces together and recruiting young, dedicated followers in clubs across the state, Soapy believed he had a chance to upset incumbent Kim Sigler. The veterans had been out of the country during the past few years and barely knew Sigler's name. But they soon heard about their fellow serviceman, Soapy.

He hadn't inherited his fortune yet and his mother wouldn't give money to the Democrats. So the Williams mortgaged their house and the couple hit the road to win the election that fall. Arnold J. Levin, with the *Detroit News* at that time, recalled: " I was the first reporter assigned to G. Mennen Williams and toured Michigan with Nancy and Mennen in an old DeSoto convertible, me holding Nancy's knitting while Mennen drove."

Soapy appeared at countless community festivals, crowned queens, made speeches, called square dances, shook hands with millions, and developed a personal popularity rarely matched in political annals.[2]

No town was too small for him to visit. He'd drop into local barber shops to talk and greet people on the street corners with his wide smile. He had a low voice and spoke slowly, almost with a drawl. He was friendly and people liked the tall, good-natured man... regardless of how liberal he was or which party he belonged to.

Martha Griffiths, who years later became the first woman to be elected lieutenant governor, helped plot strategy and get votes for Soapy. He got the black vote, too. Until 1930 most of the blacks were supporters of the Republican party, but Roosevelt's New Deal won more and more of them over to the Democrat party. It all came together when Soapy won the primary election and went on to win the gubernatorial election.

His brother Dick gave him a green and white, polka-dot bow tie for an inaugural gift and it became Soapy's trademark from then on. He kept building up his following.

He was elected five more terms as governor. Some of the elections were squeakers, but he served twelve years and set a record for holding the office for so long.

His greatest achievement was the completion of the Mackinac Bridge. He had a lot of ideas, like others before him, to improve social conditions in the state. But like others before him, he also had a legislature that went its own way and put the brakes on many of his recommendations.

He did get some cooperation, however, from the legislature by going back to his square dancing. It was in the middle of the night on May 5, 1949. The legislators had been in session since 10 o'clock in the morning and were waiting for a report so they could adjourn and go home. They were a tired and quarrelsome bunch. Soapy came in, threw off his coat and invited them to dance. A Senator played the piano, lady visitors lined up with the lawmakers and Soapy called a square dance.[3]

To his credit, Williams ran a clean and honest administration. Sigler had cleared out a lot of corruption and Soapy kept it that way. He also had an ace press secretary, Paul Weber and members of the press considered Soapy "totally dedicated to the people of Michigan." When he decided not to run for a seventh term in 1960, he was appointed assistant secretary of state for African affairs.

After five years in this post, Williams was named U.S. Ambassador to the Philippines (1968-69) and returned from Washington to his home in Grosse Pointe Farms. In 1970, Williams was elected to the State Supreme Court and re-elected for a second eight-year term before retiring in 1986.

Two years later, on February 2, 1988, Williams had a massive cerebral hemorrhage and died several hours later at the age of 76. He had an impressive military funeral and was buried in the cemetery on Mackinac Island.[4]

Governor John B. Swainson
1961 and 1962

W hen Governor John Swainson's impressionistic portrait was hung in the State Capitol Rotunda, some viewers including Swainson, wondered if the artist had finished the painting. But the hullabaloo died down, just as it had after Governor Fred Green's portrait was hung. Green is shown wearing a bright red hunting jacket, a shotgun slung across his arm and two hunting dogs at his feet.[1] People said it was not gubernatorial.

John Burley Swainson had been G. Mennen William's lieutenant governor before being elected governor in 1960. He was born in Windsor, Ontario, July 31, 1925, to John A.C. and Edna May Burley Swainson and had one brother and one sister. He was the second governor born outside the United States, Governor Fred Warner having been born in England.

The Swainson family moved to Port Huron when John was nine months old and he was raised there. He went to the public schools, became an Eagle Scout and was captain of his high school football team. He was good-looking, popular with his classmates and his future looked bright.

Upon graduating from high school, 18 year-old John became a naturalized citizen, joined the U.S. Army and was assigned as a combat infantryman to the Third Army under command of General George S. Patton, Jr. In November 1944, he volunteered to go with three others in a Jeep to deliver ammunition and other supplies to the front, near Metz, France. The Jeep hit a German land mine and exploded.[2]

Swainson, patrolling on foot, was some 15 yards away from the explosion and, although the men in the Jeep were killed instantly, he was thrown to the ground and woke up three days later in a hospital. One of his legs had been blown off below the knee and the other one was so mangled it had to be amputated at a field hospital.

He was awarded medals for his bravery and during the next 14 months he underwent a number of operations. He was sent to Percy Jones Army Hospital in Battle Creek to recuperate and get used to his artificial legs. When he was able to get around, he decided to go to nearby Olivet College.

"I decided to go to Olivet because it was small," he recalled. "With the G. I. Bill, I could have gone anywhere, but because of my disabilities, Olivet was just the right size."

It was here that he met Alice Nielsen. They were married at the close of the school year, on July 21, 1946, and both returned to campus in the fall. But that winter he was injured in a toboggan accident and had to have more surgery on one leg. He was advised to live someplace where there was no snow, so they moved to Chapel Hill, North Carolina. Swainson finished his undergraduate work there and entered law school at the University of North Carolina.

By the time he had his law degree, the couple had two sons, John Stephen and Hans Peter. They moved back to Michigan and after practicing law a few years in Detroit, they moved to Plymouth and he ran for a state senate seat. He won the election in 1954 and was re-elected two years later.

During this time the Swainsons built a home in Plymouth and he commuted by train to Lansing. They had a daughter, Kristina, on October 15, 1958, and a month later Swainson was elected lieutenant governor to serve with Governor Williams. When Williams retired from office, Swainson was elected governor and the family moved to Lansing in 1961.

Swainson was 35 when he was elected governor in 1960, the second youngest man to be elected governor and the third youngest man to serve in the office. Stevens T. Mason was 24 when he was first elected in 1836 and James Wright Gordon was 32 when he took the office in 1841. (Gordon wasn't elected, however, and became governor only because Governor William Woodbridge resigned to go to Washington.)

He had moved rapidly from the senate to the governorship, but once in the office was faced with the same problems that had faced many other governors: finances and a legislature controlled by the opposition party. Also, during his two-year term the Constitutional Convention of 1961 was taking place in Lansing. Activities in the convention, and political moves by one of its vice presidents, George Romney, overshadowed Swainson's governorship.

When the 1962 campaign rolled around, Romney was indeed the Republican candidate for governor and he won the election. Swainson, still in his 30s, returned to practice law in Detroit and was elected a Wayne County Circuit Court Judge in 1965.[3] Five years later he was elected to the Michigan Supreme Court.

By now the Swainsons had bought a large farm near Manchester and again, the future looked bright but difficult times were to follow. Swainson had served on the court for five years when he was accused of accepting a bribe and resigned under a cloud. He was found not guilty of taking the bribe, but was charged with perjury to the grand jury. He was 50 years old when he found himself without a license to practice law for three years.

It was a tough, lonesome battle, but the former governor worked hard at restoring his reputation and regained his license to practice law. By 1985 he was appointed to the Michigan Historical Commission and in later years became president of the commission.

Looking on the bright side, Swainson likes to point out that he has set another record. He's been an ex-governor longer than any other Michigan governor.

Governor George W. Romney
1963 to January 22, 1969

Throughout most of his life George Romney had to struggle against the odds. He became a successful businessman, governor of Michigan and a U.S. Cabinet member, but he still likes to battle the odds and take on a challenge.

George Wilcken Romney was only five years old when he was evacuated by train with his pregnant mother and four brothers from Chicuahaua,

Mexico. Three days later they arrived in El Paso, Texas, with 2,300 other Mormon refugees. His father walked more than 150 miles, along with 235 men, 500 horses and a commissary wagon, to join the family. They were always on guard against Pancho Villa and the Mexican rebels.

Up to now, the Mexicans had been friendly and Gaskill Romney had done well as a carpenter in Chicuahaua. His sons, Maurice, Douglas and Miles had been born there before George Wilcken's birth on July 8, 1907. A younger brother, Lawrence, was only two years old when they had to run for their lives.

The Romney family lost all but $25, two suitcases and three bedrolls. Their sixth son, Charles, was born after they arrived in El Paso and then the family moved on. Gaskell and his wife, Anna Amelia Pratt Romney, raised seven children, the six boys and one daughter, Meryl, who was born later. Lawrence died when he was 12.

Young George learned early in life that success came only with hard work. At seven, he was hoeing potatoes on the family farm outside Oakley, Utah. When he was 11, he earned his first money thinning sugar beets at a dollar an acre and shocking wheat at a dollar a day in Rexburg, Idaho.

When the family finally settled permanently in Salt Lake City, George helped in his father's construction business after classes and during summers. Although two of his brothers were on high school football teams, and one was an amateur boxing champion, George had to work at being an athlete.

He spent three years as a scrub tackle, taking a real drubbing but not giving up until he finally grew tall enough and heavy enough to make the team as a halfback. When he went out for basketball, he was on the scrub team until his junior year when he made the team as a guard. He played right field on the baseball team and finally, in his senior year, earned a letter in all three sports.

It was while George was in Latter-Day Saints University High School that he met Lenore LaFount. By the time they graduated he'd begun a courtship that was another challenge. He eventually crossed the continent seven times before he convinced her to become his wife.[1]

He spent a year in the British Isles as a missionary for the Church of Jesus Christ of Latter-Day Saints and returned to study a year at the University of Utah. By this time Lenore was in Washington, D.C., attending George Washington University. So George went to Washington, got a job and and studied at the University for two years, too. Then he began working as a tariff specialist for a senator.

Lenore moved to New York to study theater and although George had begun training as an apprentice for Alcoa Aluminum Company in Pittsburgh, he made weekend trips to see her. She went to Hollywood in 1930 and Romney managed to get a company transfer to California. She turned down a film offer and they were married in 1931.

Now that he'd made the "best sale of my life," as he described getting Lenore to marry him, Romney took on the challenge of becoming a successful businessman.[2] He transferred back to Washington with the aluminum company and after nine years he left the job to become Detroit manager of the Automobile Manufacturers Association.

The Romney family moved to Michigan in 1939, with their two daughters, Lynn and Jane. Two sons, (George) Scott and (Willard) Mitt were born during the next few years.

Then, in 1948, Romney started working for the Nash-Kelvinator Corporation, and helped arrange a merger with the Hudson Motor Car Company, to form the American Motors Corporation (AMC). He became president and chairman of AMC in 1954 and turned the money-losing company into a profit-making one.

By this time Romney was rich. He could have stayed at the job, chosen almost any other, or retired to a life of ease.[3] But he saw a need to help Detroit's schools and headed a Citizens Committee to work out their problems. It worked so well that in 1959, when the state was in a financial crisis, he helped organize the nonpartisan Citizens for Michigan.

Citizens for Michigan worked primarily for a state constitutional convention to rewrite the 53-year-old one in effect. When voters approved the convention, Romney was elected a delegate on the Republican ticket. It was no secret that he would have liked to have been elected president of the convention, but he was in the political world now and had to settle for being one of three vice presidents elected.

It wasn't long before people throughout the state began to hear about George Romney. Reporters realized he was a man of integrity and didn't fit in any mold. He was dedicated. He was determined. He resigned from AMC and ran for governor in 1962.

Romney campaigned across the state, Lenore traveled a separate route and their entire family worked with them. People liked what they saw and heard. That fall, Romney won the election. At the inaugural ball, 15 year-old Mitt was swamped with partners. He'd promised teen-age girls while traveling with his parents during the campaign that if his father won, he'd dance with them at the ball.

When Romney ran for re-election two years later, he won by a wider margin than before. He'd guided a government that was nearly bankrupt to solid financial ground and made advances in education, civil rights and treatment of the mentally ill and retarded. He fought accepting federal matching funds for Aid to Dependent Children (ADC), saying it would lead to the break-up of families.

In 1966 Romney was re-elected, this time for four years since the new State Constitution had lengthened the term of governor. Within two years, however, Romney decided to try for the U.S. Presidential nomination. He lost to Richard Nixon, but in 1969 President Nixon appointed him to his cabinet as Secretary of Housing and Urban Development (HUD).

Romney resigned the governorship and moved to Washington. While he was working there, Lenore was nominated to run for a seat in the U.S. Senate from Michigan. She campaigned hard but lost the election and spent the rest of her time with him in the nation's capitol until he resigned his post with HUD in February 1973.

The Romneys returned to their home in Bloomfield Hills and he became a consultant with an international accounting firm. In 1993, at age 86, Romney is doing what he has always believed in, getting people to help each other rather than depending on the government to make this a better world. As honorary chairman of the Michigan Campaign for Volunteerism, he says "People solve the problems. Money helps, but money by itself can't do a blessed thing."

Governor William G. Milliken
1969 through 1982

Lieutenant Governor William Milliken became Governor when George Romney resigned to go to Washington as a member of the President's Cabinet. When the next election came up, Milliken was elected to the office on his own... the first Lt. Governor in the history of Michigan to do this. Two others who had stepped up when a governor resigned, Andrew Parsons and Loren Dickinson, tried to win the next election for governor but were defeated.

Milliken's grandfather and father had both been state senators and although it took him almost 37 years before he got into politics, he took to it like a duck to water. He did so well, in fact, that he was in office for 14 years and set a record as Michigan's longest- serving governor.

William Grawn Milliken was born in Traverse City on March 26, 1922, and he was raised there with his older brother, John, who became a physician, and a younger sister, Ruth. His grandfather, James W. Milliken, founded a department store in Traverse City and served in the Michigan Senate. His father, James T. Milliken, continued to run the family store and also served in the state senate. His mother, Hildegarde, was a University of Michigan graduate who preferred the word statesman, rather than politician.

Young Bill's parents were strict with their children and held them to high standards. He was not allowed to go out on week nights, studied for an hour each school night, and had to be in on weekends at a time set by his parents. He had to keep his room clean, take care of the lawn, and only on special occasions was he allowed to drive the family car.[1]

While a student at Traverse City High School, Bill was into everything. He was president of his freshman class, on the school newspaper staff, an extempore speaker for his school, in band and orchestra, and earned letters in tennis, basketball and track. Although he wasn't a star, he was on the basketball team the year they won the Class B State Championship in 1940.[2]

He also was on the student council and elected school governor. He liked student government and this interest led him into a correspondence with former Governor Chase S. Osborn. The Osborns were friends of his parents and Gov. Osborn encouraged Bill to go into politics. When he answered Bill's letters, he put a $1 bill in them. "I saved his letters and I should have also saved the dollars," Milliken had fun saying in later years.

Although he worked part-time for spending money by packing and sweeping floors at the family store during the school year, during summers he worked full-time. He pumped gas 50 hours a week for $8 at a Sinclair station. He used some of his hard-earned money to buy a car with his brother. They found a Ford Phaeton four-door convertible for

$200 in Detroit. It was custom-built, had a chrome dashboard and six horns run by three separate buttons. It also had a flat tire on the way back home to Traverse City.

Bill visited several colleges while in high school and decided on Yale University, his father's alma mater. In the fall of 1940, after graduating from high school, Bill left for the university at New Haven, Connecticut. In his freshman year he was on the basketball and track teams. When he was a sophomore he earned his letter in basketball, but by then the country was in World War II and things were changing fast. Classes were being held during the summer so students could graduate in less time.

By February 1943, Milliken had completed his junior year and gone into active service in the U.S. Army Air Force. Part of his training was in aerial gunnery school at Lowry Field in Denver, Colorado. It was here that he met Helen Wallbank and they dated all summer until she returned to Smith College for her junior year.

Bill was sent to Italy, where he flew fifty combat missions in ten months as a B-24 waist gunner. He survived a crash on take off with a full bomb load. On another mission, his plane made a crash landing in a field. On one flight over Austria, he was wounded in the stomach by flak. On another mission he bailed out over Italy when his crippled plane, its hydraulic system shot out, ran out of gas 50 miles from its base.[3] He was awarded many medals, including the Air Medal with two Bronze Oak Leaf Clusters and a Purple Heart. He was also lucky. The average life of a waist gunner in combat during the war was about five minutes.

Soon after returning from the service, Bill and Helen were married and they went back to New Haven so he could finish his senior year and graduate from Yale. Then they returned to Michigan and he began working in the family's department store in Traverse City because his father needed his help. Their two children, William, Jr., and Elaine were born in Traverse City.

When his father died in 1952, Bill became president of J.W. Milliken, Inc. and began an expansion program which included adding two more stores. For the next eight years he planned, worked and worried until he'd raised the companies annual sales of $400,000 to $2,000,000.

Then, in 1960, Milliken decided to run for a seat in the Michigan Senate.

He won the election and led some hard fought battles to bring a more moderate philosophy into the majority of the Republican party. He looked very young, but the senators soon learned he was a tough opponent.

Milliken could disagree with people without disliking them. They liked him back. He had a quiet sense of humor and was always courteous to those who worked with him or for him. No one took advantage of him, though. He was firm and if displeased, it showed in his eyes. Reporters were impressed with his integrity.

He was re-elected to the Senate in 1962. Many of the progessive programs he'd promoted were adopted and made popular by newly elected Governor George Romney. By the next election in 1964, Milliken decided to make a bid for Lt. Governor on the ticket with Romney and he won. At first Romney didn't delegate authority to Milliken, but gradually the two began to work well together and trust each other.

In 1966, the new Constitution required the governor and lieutenant governor be elected jointly for four year terms. Governor Romney made it a point to be neutral in the selection of his Lt. Governor and Milliken earned the nomination himself. They were elected as a team. When Romney decided to campaign for the presidential nomination, Milliken acted as governor for many days and weeks. But Romney withdrew from the race and Richard Nixon was elected.

When Governor Romney accepted the post of Secretary of Housing and Urban Development in Washington, Milliken became governor on January 22, 1969. He cited a balanced budget, quality environment and education as major issues facing the legislature.

In the fall of 1970, Milliken ran for his own term as governor. He won a narrow victory and faced some serious problems during the next four years, primarily the threat of PBB in food products. A chemical fire retardant, PBB had been accidently mixed in dry food for cattle and got into the food chain. The danger to humans was unknown but the cattle themselves died or were born deformed after eating the feed. Thousands of cows were killed to keep the chemical from spreading into milk and milk products. It was a disaster for the farmers and an alarming situation for the people.

But Milliken handled the situation as well as possible and was re-elected in 1974 by a larger margin than before. Other crises arose. There was an oil embargo by the Arabs that caused a shortage of gasoline and a dip in the economy. But again in 1978, Milliken was re-elected and continued to work with a Democrat controlled legislature.

He was criticized for his stand on several issues, such as providing financial help to Detroit, but he stood firm for the things he believed were right. At the close of his 14 years as governor he did not run again for the office.

Milliken, with a friendly grin and steadfastness of purpose, left office with many friends and few enemies. He had proved that a gentleman can be effective. "I don't believe civility is a sign of weakness," he'd said and he proved it.

There were many opportunities for him to run for other government offices, such as the U.S. Senate. But Bill Milliken was devoted to being a good governor of Michigan and not interested in any other political job. When he left the governorship he went into new fields.

He served as founding chairman of the Center for the Great Lakes, served on boards such as the Ford Foundation and the Interlochen Center for the Arts. Busy as ever today, Milliken enjoys life and is a contented man.

Governor James J. Blanchard
1983 through 1990

T hat boy is going to be governor of Michigan someday," James
Blanchard's uncle told his mother. But young Jamie dreamed of
becoming a U.S. Congressman when he grew up and he did. Then
he become the governor.

James (or Jamie) Johnston Blanchard was born in Detroit on August 8,
1942. He had one sister, Suzanne, who was four years older and they led

normal, happy lives when they were small. His mother and father were both graduates of Ohio State University.[1]

His father, James R., was a research metallurgist and his mother, Rosalie Johnston Blanchard Webb, had her degree in education. They took the children with them when they traveled on his job and they saw a lot of the country. But when Jamie was a 9-year-old, his father was depressed and needed some time alone. His mother took the children to visit her mother-in-law in Ohio and when they returned they found that his father had moved out of their house in Ferndale and left for good.

His mother worked as a receptionist for a doctor and raised the children alone for several years. She remarried when Jamie was a sophomore in high school, but her husband died three-and-a-half years later. Then she worked in the Oakland County Social Services Department.

As a boy, Jamie wanted to grow up and be a baseball player. He idolized the Detroit Tigers and Al Kaline, in particular. He would hang around Tiger Stadium and ride his bicycle past the home of outfielder Kaline, hoping to get a glimpse of him. Naturally, he collected baseball cards.

When he was 10, Jamie started dropping into a Democratic party headquarters around the corner from their house. They paid him 50 cents an hour to hang party leaflets on doorknobs in the neighborhood. It was a highlight in his life when he got to go as a page to the National Democratic Convention and met leading candidates, including Adlai Stevenson. Then he collected clippings about politicians, put them in scrapbooks and saved them all his life.

As his interest in becoming a big league baseball player faded, Jamie turned all his drive and energy toward politics. He was elected president of his freshman high school class and president of the 1959 Ferndale High School Student Council when he was a senior. He went out for track when he was a senior and earned his letter, but he was focused on student government.

His mother encouraged Jamie to run for elective offices because she had been raised in a family that was active in politics. Her brother had made an unsuccessful bid for lieutenant governor of Ohio and her mother, a crusader for women's rights, had served on the local school board.

By the time he entered Michigan State University, Blanchard was familiar with the political process. When he was a sophomore he ran a smooth campaign and was elected president of his class. By the time he was a senior, he had built up his own organization and followers. He was again elected president of his class.

Outgoing, friendly and diplomatic, Blanchard was a big man on campus. He met another student, Paula Parker of Clarkston, Michigan, and she too was interested in student government. They were married a week after she graduated in June 1966, and he had finished his first year at the University of Minnesota Law School. She didn't realize that he was so completely dedicated to politics until their wedding. She wrote later. "Jamie was scanning the audience and…that was my first glimpse of what it was going to be like to be a politician's wife."[2]

When Blanchard completed work on his law degree in 1968, the couple moved to Lansing and he worked in the State Attorney General's office. Their only child, Jay, was born on October 1, 1970.

Four years later Blanchard was elected to the U.S. Congress and they moved to Washington, D.C. He was re-elected every two years and represented Michigan for a total of eight years. During this time he was instrumental in getting a loan for Chrysler Corporation from the federal government and his name became familiar throughout Michigan.

Deciding the time was ripe for a Democrat to win a gubernatorial election in Michigan, Blanchard mustered his forces and became the party's candidate in 1982. His friend and former employer, Attorney General Frank Murphy, brought the factions in the Democrat party together. Labor and regular Democrats had been fighting among themselves, but they united behind Blanchard and he won the election.

As governor he had a Democratic legislature to work with for a short time. They increased the income tax and two of the legislators were recalled, leaving him with a Republican-controlled senate and things didn't go so smoothly for him then. However, by the time the next election (1986) rolled around, Michigan's economy had improved and he was re-elected.

Six months after his second term was underway, Paula filed for a divorce. This was the first gubernatorial divorce in Michigan history and created a lot of publicity, but Blanchard continued his work as before. He married Janet Fox on September 2, 1989 and began his campaign for a third term in 1990.

Things just didn't go right this time around. Martha Griffiths, his 78-year-old lieutenant governor was not happy when he picked another running-mate and kicked up a storm. Paula had written a book, "Til Politics Do Us Part," which was published a few months before the election and may not have hurt his chances, but didn't help them either.

There was also a "throw the rascals out" feeling among voters which resulted in 14 governors being turned out of office in the fall and Blanchard was one of them. He left office saying he felt a burden had been lifted from his shoulders, although he would have liked to have completed some of the projects he had initiated for the good of the state.

The Blanchards kept a residence in Beverly Hills, Michigan, but moved to Washington, D.C. where he became a highly-paid consultant for a law firm. They helped William J. Clinton during his presidential campaign and afterward, Janet worked as an assistant in the presidential personnel office.

On May 27, 1993, Blanchard was nominated by President Clinton to serve as U.S. ambassador to Canada. Janet quit her job in the White House and they began studying French in preparation for the new post. The senate confirmed his appointment and on August 10th, Blanchard took the oath of office for his new job in Canada.

"His goal in life was to be a congressman and he always said the rest of his life would be an adventure," his mother recalled. Still, Blanchard's interest in politics remains strong. As he told the Senate Foreign Relations Committee earlier, on July 20, 1993, "It would be unwise and unrealistic, given my age (50), to swear off ever running for elected office again."[3]

Governor John M. Engler
1991-

L ike all farm boys, John Engler learned about hard work in the hot
sun when he was young. His parents owned a 600-acre cattle
feeding operation near Beal City, five miles from Mt. Pleasant in
central Michigan.

"When John was a 15 year-old he worked 16 hours a day on our farm,"
his mother recalls. "Up at 4 a.m. in the morning, he'd work until
midnight harvesting corn or silage and hay."[1]

"He was also very determined," she added. "He was very precise. Everything had to be right." He carried these characteristics on through his life and they didn't leave much room for fun or a sense of humor. He was taught that right was right and wrong was wrong.

John Mathias Engler was the oldest in a family of seven children. He was born on October 12, 1948 to Matt and Agnes Engler. Two brothers and four sisters soon followed and a lot was expected of him from the time he was a little boy.

Young John loved to read and especially liked history and civics (government). As he grew older, he often read the morning newspaper before catching his school bus. He was a good all-around student.

In high school John played football. "It was the first time Beal High School had a football team and half the parents wouldn't let their sons go out for it," his mother said. "They lost all their games."

She also recalled that John had a football injury. "He hadn't said much about it at the time, but later we noticed that when he bumped his arm he jumped. We took him to a doctor and found he had a calcium growth in his arm." He played the last game, though, and when he had surgery to remove the growth it was the size of a fist.

John was active in his local 4H Club at an early age and showed cattle for his project. He won boxes of ribbons for his Herefords, Angus and Charolais beef cattle. Although he never won a grand championship himself, he helped his brothers and sisters so that in 11 years the family had five grand champions in the county fairs.

As he grew older he was a member of the Future Farmers of America (FFA) and was soon a leader in the state organization.

Meanwhile, John graduated from high school and entered Michigan State University. To put himself through college he worked at the beef barn and for a time at the Agricultural Extension Office. "He also ran a hot dog stand but one year of that was enough," his mother recalled. "He was a kind of an entrepreneur."

When he was a sophomore his father, Matt, entered the 1968 primary election against incumbent Rep. Russell H. Strange, for a chance to represent the Republican party that fall in the election for a seat in the

State House of Representatives. John helped his father as much as he could, but found the campaign disorganized and without a plan. Matt Engler lost the election, but John learned a lot about politics.

In 1969, when he was a junior, John was elected president of his East Shaw Hall dormitory and tasted his first political victory. It put a new light on his father's defeat and he hadn't forgotten. The next year, two months before he graduated, he wrote a term paper for his political science class telling how to win an election against incumbent Rep. Russell H. Strange.[2]

After graduating with a degree in Agricultural Economics, 21 year-old Engler put his plan into action. It called for "perspiration and participation," and he was again working from dawn until midnight. This time, though, he wasn't pitching hay. He was shaking hands and talking to the people in his district.

His hard work and planned organization paid off. Engler defeated Rep. Strange by 159 votes in 1970 and at 22, became the youngest member in the Michigan House of Representatives. About this time he was asked how far he intended to go and he replied that he guessed he'd settle for being governor. No one paid much attention. Two years later, after districts were changed based on the U.S. Census, he ran against and defeated another incumbent and was re-elected in 1974.

Engler helped politically ambitious Colleen House from Bay City win a special election from her district in June of 1974 and they were married in 1975. They were the only husband-wife team in the legislature and sat at adjoining desks on the House chamber in the capitol.

After winning another term in the House, Engler decided to try for a senate seat in 1978. Again, he took on an incumbent and again, he won. This time he became a state senator by 1,756 votes and by now people were beginning to pay attention. He was well on his way to becoming a leader in the Republican party.

Although politics was his passion, Engler spent some of his time attending Cooley Law School in Lansing and received his law degree in 1984. His personal life changed too, when he and Colleen were divorced after 12 years of marriage.

By 1990, Engler was ready to take on Governor Jim Blanchard who was making his bid for a third term. He revised and enlarged his plan for defeating an incumbent and went to work.

During his campaign he met Michelle DeMunbrun of Texas, who was a lawyer with a happy personality and they fell in love. It wasn't until after he won the election in November, that they announced their engagement. They were married in San Antonio, Texas, on December 8, 1990 and returned to Michigan for his inauguration on January 1, 1991.

Engler had made promises to cut spending and lower property taxes while running for governor. Once in office, he cut spending so much that there was a great hue and cry from many sources. But, as one reporter pointed out, if people had listened to him they would know he was just carrying out the things he'd promised to do if he got elected.

He faced a tougher battle in getting property taxes lowered, but again, his luck and determination were underestimated. He got some unexpected help from a Democrat who introduced an amendment to do away with school property taxes. That was all he needed. He gave his blessing to it and the bill was passed by the legislature.

This was the biggest tax cut in the history of the state and left school financing in a temporary quandary. But there was no question about Governor Engler keeping his word.

Did You Know...

Michigan got its name from early Indians who called it Mishigamaw, meaning "Great Water."

Nine Michigan counties were known as "Cabinet Counties." They were named for President Andrew Jackson and members of his cabinet: Barry, Berrien, Branch, Cass, Eaton, Ingham, Jackson, Livingston and Van Buren.

Three Michigan counties were named for Governors: Alger, Luce and Mason.

All but two of Michigan's deceased governors are buried in this state. The two are Wilber M. Brucker of Detroit and James Wright Gordon of Marshall. Brucker, a U.S. Secretary of the Army, is buried in Arlington National Cemetery, Virginia. Gordon was a consul in Brazil when he died from a fall off a second-story balcony. Despite a search in recent years, no one knows where he is buried.

The Catholepistemiad of Michigania was the first name of the University of Michigan when it was established in Detroit, 1817. Governor Cass couldn't even pronounce it and referred to it as the "Cathole-what's its name." Four years later the name was simplified to University of Michigan and in 1841 it was moved to Ann Arbor.

The Republican Party was formed in Jackson, on July 6, 1854.

Four Michigan Governors were orphans. Five governors were raised by only one parent, their mother or father having died or left when they were young.

Michigan had 13 governors before one was born in Michigan. The 14th governor, David H. Jerome, was born in Detroit. All the previous ones were born in other states. Actually of Michigan's 44 governors, 32 have been born in others states and only 12 have been native Michiganians.

More than half of Michigan governors (24) have been lawyers; 11 were businessmen/ lumbermen, 4 farmers, 1 engineer, 1 publisher and 1 in government service.

Governors are elected in November but take office in January the following year. This explains why a governor may be elected in 1990, but his term of office is from 1991 through 1994.

Five former governors died while G. Mennen Williams was governor, 1949 through 1960. They were Republicans Kim Sigler, Chase S. Osborn, Alexander J. Groesbeck, and Democrats William A. Comstock and Frank Murphy.

Endnotes

If you'd like to know more about Michigan's governors, the books listed below will give you details. If you're interested in learning about the governors' wives, you'll want to read, "First Ladies of Michigan," Revised second edition, by Willah Weddon.

Governor Stevens T. Mason
1. Claudius B. Grant, *Messages of the Governors of Michigan*, Michigan Historical Commission, Vol. II, Lansing, 1926, p.115.
2. *Michigan Biographies*, Volume II, Michigan Historical Commission, Lansing, 1924, p.84.
3. F. Clever Bald, *Michigan In Four Centuries*, Harper and Brothers, 1961, p.191.
4. Willis Dunbar, *Michigan: A History of the Wolverine State*, 1965, p.303
5. Grant, Ibid. p.116.
6. Dunbar, Ibid. p.346.
7. Jean Frazier, *Michigan History Magazine*, January/February issue, 1980, p.31.

Governor William Woodbridge
1. Emily George, R.S.M., *William Woodbridge, Michigan's Connecticut Yankee*, Michigan History Division, Michigan Department of State, from his address to the New England Society of Michigan, Dec. 22, 1847, p.76.
2. Burke A. Hinsdale, *History of the University of Michigan*, 1906, p.166.

Governor James Wright Gordon
1. Michigan Pioneer Collection XI, 1887, p.274.
2. *Representative Men of Michigan*, Michigan volume of the American Biographical History of Eminent and Self-Made Men, Western Biographical Publishing Co., 1878, p.38.
3. Charles Lanman, *The Red Book of Michigan*, E.B. Smith and Co., Detroit, 1871, p.274.
4. Jerry Roe, Member Michigan Historical Commission, Lansing, 1993, in discussion with the author.

Governor John S. Barry
1. Sue I. Silliman, *A Prince in Puddleford*, Three Rivers, p.263.

Governor Alpheus Felch
1. Claudius B. Grant, *Messages of the Governors of Michigan*, Vol. 11, The Michigan Historical Commission, Lansing, 1926, p.13-14.
2. *Representative Men of Michigan*, Michigan volume of the American Biographical History of Eminent and Self-Made Men, Western Biographical Publishing Co., 1878, p.35.

Governor William L. Greenly
1. Burke A. Hinsdale, *History of the University of Michigan*, 1906, p.168.
2. Henry Utley, *Michigan as Province, Territory, State*, Vol.3, p.280.
3. *Michigan Biographies*, Volume 1, Michigan Historical Commission, Lansing, 1924, p.351.

Governor Epaphroditus Ransom
1. Wyllys Cadwell Ransom, *Ransom Family of America*, Cochester Branch, Richmond and Backus, Ann Arbor, 1903, p.98 and 99.
2. Arthur A. Hagman, Editor, *Oakland County Book of History*, 1970, p.97.
3. Pamphlet honoring Epaphroditus Ransom, Local History section, Kalamazoo Public Library.
4. *Kalamazoo Daily Telegraph*, March 19, 1877.

Governor Robert McClelland
1. Charles R. Tuttle, *General History of the States*, History of Michigan, 1878, p.427.
2. *Representative Men of Michigan*, Michigan volume, American Biographical History of Eminent and Self-Made Men, Western Biographical Publishing Co., 1878, p.104.

Governor Andrew Parsons
1. *Michigan Biographies*, Volume 1, Michigan Historical Commission, Lansing, 1924, p.513.
2. Charles Lanman, *The Red Book of Michigan*, E.B. Smith and Co., Detroit 1871, p.473 and 474.

Birth of a Party
1. Linda Braun-Hass, Jackson—*Birthplace of the Republican Party*, Vantage Press, 1991, p.12.
2. Jerry Roe, Lansing, Member of the Michigan Historical Commission.

Governor Kinsley S. Bingham
1. Linda Braun-Hass, Jackson—*Birthplace of the Republican Party*, Vantage Press, 1991, p.35.

Governor Moses Wisner
1.Ruth G. Priestley, *The Moses Wisner Family*, Part I, Oakland Gazette, November 1974.
2. *Representative Men of Michigan*, Michigan volume, American Biographical History of Eminent and Self-Made Men, Western Biographical Publishing Co., 1878, p.80.

Governor Austin Blair
1. *Representative Men of Michigan*, Michigan volume, American Biographical History of Eminent and Self-Made Men, Western Biographical Publishing Co., 1878, p.11.
2. Nellie Blair Greene, *Historic Jackson County*, No. 26, The Austin Blair Home, Part II, p.1.
3. *Early History of Michigan Biographies*, S.D. Bingham, 1888, p.106.

Governor Henry H.Crapo
1. *The New Bedford (Massachusetts) Standard*, reprinted in Flint's *Wolverine Citizen*, August 7, 1869, p.4.
2. *Representative Men of Michigan*, Michigan volume, American Biographical History of Eminent and Self-Made Men, Western Biographical Publishing Co., 1878, p.34.
3. *The Wolverine Citizen*, Flint, July 24, 1869, p.4.

Governor Henry P. Baldwin
1. Arthur A. Hagman, Editor, *Oakland County Book of History*, 1978, p.101.
2. George Weeks, *Stewards of the State: The Governors of Michigan*, The Detroit News and the Historical Society of Michigan, 1991, p.50.

Governor John J. Bagley
1. Robert Sobel and John Raimo, editors, *Biographical Directory of the Governors of the United States: 1789-1978*, 1978, p.750.
2. Charles A. Weissert, Gazette Historian, *Kalamazoo Gazette*, August 31, 1947.
3. Henry Utley, *Michigan as Province, Territory, State*, Vol. 4, 1906, p.110.

Governor Charles M. Croswell
1. *Michigan Manual*, 1877, p.635 and 636.
2. Adrian Woman's Club, Ninetieth Anniversary booklet, May 20, 1973.
3. *Biographies of Pioneers, Governors of Michigan*, 1880, p.162
4. *Adrian Daily Telegram*, Nov. 1, 1961.

Governor David H. Jerome
1. Jerome Genealogy, compiled by Elizabeth Jerome Brigati.
2. Arthur A. Hagman, Editor, *Oakland County Book of History*, 1978, p.107.
3. *Portrait and Biographical Album of Jackson County Michigan*, Chapman Brothers, Chicago, Illinois, May 1890.
4. Willis Dunbar, Michigan: *A History of the Wolverine State*, 1965, p.481.

Governor Josiah W. Begole
1. *Representative Men of Michigan*, Michigan volume, Western Biographical Publishing Co., 1878, p.9.
2. Robert Sobel and John Raimo, editors, *Biographical Directory of the Governors of the United States: 1789-1978*, 1978.

Governor Russell A. Alger
1. *Founders and Makers of Michigan*, Memorial Society of Michigan, Inc., S. J. Clarke Publishing Co., Inc., Detroit and Indianapolis, p.285.
2. Adj. Gen. John Robertson, *Michigan in the War*, p. 760.
3. *Representative Men of Michigan*, Michigan volume, Western Biographical Publishing Co., 1878, p.3.
4. *Founders and Makers of Michigan*, Ibid., p.285.

Governor Cyrus G. Luce
1. *Kalamazoo Daily Telegraph*, November 9, 1888.
2. *In Memory of Hon. Cyrus Gray Luce*, published by authority of the Michigan Legislature of 1905, p.82.
3. Ibid. p.85.
4. *The Courier and Republican*, Coldwater, March 20, 1905, p.1.

Governor Edwin B. Winans
1. Claudius B. Grant, *Governors of the Territory and State of Michigan*, Michigan Historical Commission, Lansing, 1928.
2. Howard Hovey, *Livingston County Republican-Press*, Howell, July 1, 1936, p.5.
3. Ibid.

Governor John T. Rich
1. Sam Painter, Davison, information to the author, July 1977 and October 1992.
2. *Detroit Free Press*, March 29, 1926.
   Also see *Governor John T. Rich*, by Former Justice Joseph B. Moore, Lansing, Michigan State Library vertical file.

Governor Hazen S. Pingree
1. Arthur Hagman, Editor, *Oakland County Book of History*, 1970, p.105.
2. Melvin G. Holli, *Mayor Pingree Campaigns for the Governorship,* Michigan History, Vol. 64, No. l, January-February 1980, p.38.
3. F. Clever Bald, *Michigan in Four Centuries*, Harper and Brothers, New York, 1961, p.332.
4. Ibid, p.334.
5. Willis Dunbar, *Michigan: A History of the Wolverine State*, 1965, p.535.

Governor Aaron T. Bliss
1. *Mid York Weekly,* Aaron T. Bliss, the Soldier, Part I. Copied by Ethyl D. Tarr.
2. George Walker, Chips and Shavings, *Mid York Weekly*, Hamilton, New York.
3. Ibid.
4. *Detroit Free Press*, September 17, 1906.

Governor Fred M. Warner
1. Jean M. Fox, *"I Went to the People… "* Fred M. Warner: Progressive Governor, Farmington Hills Historical Commission, 1988, p.8.
2. F. Clever Bald, *Michigan in Four Centuries,* Harper and Brothers, New York, 1961, p.339.

Governor Chase S. Osborn
1. George Weeks, *Stewards of the State: The Governors of Michigan*, The Detroit News and the Historical Society of Michigan, 1991, p.76.
2. F. Clever Bald, *Michigan in Four Centuries,* Harper and Brothers, New York, 1961, p.336.
3. Stella B. Osborn, *An Accolade for Chase S. Osborn*, City of Sault Ste. Marie, 1939.
4. Detroit Magazine, *Detroit Free Press*, September 21, 1986, p.13.

Governor Woodbridge N. Ferris
1. John Fitzgibbon, *Senator Ferris and His Career*, Detroit News, March 24, 1918.
2. *Michigan Biographies*, Volume 1, Michigan Historical Commission, Lansing, 1924, p.288.

Governor Albert E. Sleeper
1. Clark Herrington, M.D., Bad Axe, from Mary Sleeper's Diaries, 1993.
2. Margaret Eccles, "The Political Career of Albert E. Sleeper," Master's thesis, Wayne State University, 1941.
3. F. Clever Bald, *Michigan in Four Centuries*, Harper and Brothers, New York, 1961, p.375.
4. Jerry Roe, Lansing, Michigan Historical Commission member, 1993.

Governor Alexander J. Groesbeck
1. Thomas E. Brown, *Michigan History*, Vol. 64, No. 1, p.40.
2. Willis Dunbar, *Michigan: The Wolverine State*, 1965, p.635.
3. Frank M. Sparks, 160,000 Majority Is Hard For Even Green to Believe, *Grand Rapids Herald*, Sept. 17, 1926.

Governor Fred W. Green
1. Guy H. Jenkins, Lansing Bureau Chief, *Kalamazoo Gazette*, May 9, 1954, State Page.
2. George N. Fuller, Editor, *Messages of the Governors of Michigan*, Vol. 4, pp 855-6.
3. Jenkins, Ibid.
   Also see *James Oliver Curwood*, Bowling Green State University Press, 1993, by Judith A. Eldridge.

Governor Wilber M. Brucker
1. *Lansing State Journal*, UPI report from Detroit, June 14, 1955.
2. Ben Price, AP Newsfeature writer, *Grand Rapids Herald*, September 18, 1955.
3. *Flint Journal*, Associated Press report, June 22, 1955.

Governor William A. Comstock
1. John P. White, *The Governor of Michigan as Party Leader: The Case of William A. Comstock*, Papers of the Michigan Academy of Science, Arts and Letters, Vol. XLII, 1957, pp 193-94.
2. William Muller, Death Ends Comstock's Long Career, *Detroit News*, June 17, 1949.
3. White, Ibid., p.189.
4. *Detroit News*, June 24, 1932.

Governor John D. Fitzgerald
1. Frank M. Fitzgerald (Fitzgerald's grandson), *A Remembrance of Governor Fitzgerald of Grand Ledge*, Grand Ledge Area Historical Society, 1985, p.8 and 12.
2. Dick Frazier, *Lansing State Journal*, January 27, 1985.

Governor Frank Murphy
1. Clifford A. Prevost, Washington Bureau, *Detroit Free Press*, October 16, 1951.
2. Sidney Fine, *Frank Murphy: A Michigan Life*, Historical Society of Michigan, 1985, p.4-5.
3. Denise Bancroft, Lansing, (Niece of Marguerite Murphy Teahan), correspondence with author, August 1992.

Governor Luren Dickinson
1. Don Lochbiler, Staff writer, *Detroit News*.
2. Governor Luren D. Dickinson: autobiography, manuscript, 1939, p.2.
3. D. L. Runnells, Sept. 28, 1938
4. Lochbiler, Ibid.

Governor Murray D. Van Wagoner
1. Steve Spilos, *East Detroiter*.
2. James M. Haswell, Lansing Correspondent, *Detroit Free Press*, Dec. 29, 1931.
3. Earl Dowdy, Staff writer, *Detroit News*, June 13, 1986.

Governor Harry F. Kelly
1. *Detroit News* Obituary, June 2, 1971.
2. Michigan History Magazine, Winter 1943, p.7.
3. William O'Briend Marion (Kelly's nephew), Michigan History Magazine, Vol. 25, No.2, Fall 1989, p.2.
4. Willard Baird, *State Journal* Capitol Bureau, Dec. 25, 1970.

Governor Kim Sigler
1. Kendrick Kimball, *Detroit News Pictorial*, January 19, 1947, p.13.
2. Morgan Oates, Free Press Librarian, "Our Flamboyant Cowboy Governor," *Detroit Free Press Sunday Magazine*, January 13, 1963.
3. *Lansing State Journal*, December 1, 1953.

Governor G. Mennen Williams
1. Frank McNaughton, *Mennen Williams of Michigan*, Oceana Publicaions, Inc., N.Y., 1960, p.5.
2. Willis Dunbar, *Michigan: A History of the Wolverine State*, 1965, p.655.
3. F. Clever Bald, *Michigan in Four Centuries*, 1961, p.453.
4. Nancy Williams Gram, Grosse Pointe Farms, conversation with the author, July 10, 1993.

Governor John B. Swainson
1. Roger Lane, Lansing Staff, *Detroit Free Press*, March 9, 1965.
2. George Weeks, *Stewards of the State: The Governors of Michigan*, 1991, p.117.
3. Arthur A. Hagman, Editor, *Oakland County Book of History*, 1970, p.114.

Governor George W. Romney
1. George Romney, correspondence with author, 1992.
2. George Weeks, *Stewards of the State: The Governors of Michigan*, 1991, p.120.
3. Ernest Havenmann, The George Romney Family, *Ladies Home Journal*, October 1966.

Governor William G. Milliken
1. Dan Angel, *William G. Milliken: A Touch of Steel*, Public Affairs Press, Warren, Mich., 1970, p.20.
2. Ibid., p.25.
3. Joyce Braithwaite and George Weeks, *The Milliken Years: A Pictorial Reflection*, The Village Press, Inc., and the Traverse City Record-Eagle, 1988, p.23.

Governor James J. Blanchard
1. Rosalie Blanchard Webb, South Lyon, in a telephone interview with the author, July 20, 1993. Information and quotes, unless otherwise noted, are from Mrs. Webb.
2. Paula Blanchard, *Til Politics Do Us Part*, A & M Publishing Co., Inc., West Bloomfield Hills, Michigan, 1990.
3. *Jackson Citizen Patriot*, Associated Press report, July 21, 1993.

Governor John M. Engler

1. Mrs. Agnes Engler , Mt. Pleasant, in a telephone interview with the author, July 17, 1993. Information and quotes, unless otherwise noted, are from Mrs. Engler.
2. Roger Martin, Nolan Finley, George Weeks and The Detroit News Lansing Bureau: Charlie Cain, Mark Hornbeck and Yolanda Woodlee, *The Journey of John Engler*, A & M Publishing Co., Inc., 1991, p.8.

Special thanks to Virginia Hutcheson, East Lansing, who opened her research files to the author.

Governors of the State of Michigan

Governor	Party Affiliation	Years in Office
John M. Engler	Republican	1991-
James J. Blanchard	Democrat	1983-1990
William G. Milliken	Republican	1969-1982
George W. Romney	Republican	1963-1969
John B. Swainson	Democrat	1961-1962
G. Mennen Williams	Democrat	1949-1960
Kim Sigler	Republican	1947-1948
Harry F. Kelly	Republican	1943-1946
Murray D. Van Wagoner	Democrat	1941-1942
Luren D. Dickinson	Republican	1939-1940
Frank D. Fitzgerald	Republican	1939
Frank Murphy	Democrat	1937-1938
Frank D. Fitzgerald	Republican	1935-1936
William A. Comstock	Democrat	1933-1934
Wilber M. Brucker	Republican	1931-1932
Fred W. Green	Republican	1927-1930
Alexander J. Groesbeck	Republican	1921-1926
Albert E. Sleeper	Republican	1917-1920
Woodbridge N. Ferris	Democrat	1913-1916
Chase S. Osborn	Republican	1911-1912
Fred M. Warner	Republican	1905-1910
Aaron T. Bliss	Republican	1901-1904
Hazen S. Pingree	Republican	1897-1900

Governors of the State of Michigan

Governor	Party Affiliation	Years in Office
John T. Rich	Republican	1893-1896
Edwin B. Winans	Democrat	1891-1892
Cyrus G. Luce	Republican	1887-1890
Russell A. Alger	Republican	1885-1886
Josiah W. Begole	Fusion	1883-1884
David H. Jerome	Republican	1881-1882
Charles M. Croswell	Republican	1877-1880
John J. Bagley	Republican	1873-1876
Henry P. Baldwin	Republican	1869-1872
Henry H. Crapo	Republican	1865-1868
Austin Blair	Republican	1861-1864
Moses Wisner	Republican	1859-1860
Kinsley S. Bingham	Republican	1855-1858
Andrew Parsons	Democrat	1853-1854
Robert McClelland	Democrat	1852-1853
John S. Barry	Democrat	1850-1851
Epaphroditus Ransom	Democrat	1848-1849
William L. Greenly	Democrat	1847
Alpheus Felch	Democrat	1846-1847
John S. Barry	Democrat	1842-1845
James W. Gordon	Whig	1841
William Woodbridge	Whig	1840-1841
Stevens T. Mason	Democrat	1835-1839

About the Author

Willah Weddon is a Michigan native with a B.A. degree from Western Michigan University and graduate credits from the University of Michigan. She did some writing for the *Kalamazoo Gazette* while in high school, wrote for the college newspaper, published the *Comstock Coronet* and was Willow Run editor for the Ypsilanti Press. She was a correspondent for the *Jackson Citizen Patriot*, *Lansing State Journal*, and *Detroit Free Press* before establishing the Women's News Bureau at the Capitol.

Weddon is a past president of the Michigan Press Women, a past secretary of the National Federation of Press Women, Inc., and a past president of the Michigan State Medical Auxiliary. She has been awarded more than 80 first place state awards and 13 national awards for writing, photography, public relations, and editing.

"Michigan Governors: Their Life Stories" joins two companion works by Weddon, "Michigan Governors Growing Up" and "First Ladies of Michigan".